Studio Stories

Studio Stories

Illuminating Our Lives through Art

Lauren Rader

Shanti Arts Publishing

Brunswick Maine

Studio Stories
Illuminating Our Lives through Art

Published by Shanti Arts Publishing
Designed by the author
Cover designed by Mayfly Design

Shanti Arts LLC
193 Hillside Road
Brunswick, Maine 04011
shantiarts.com

Printed in the United States of America

ISBN: 978-1-941830-50-5 (hardcover)
ISBN: 978-1-941830-89-5 (softcover)
ISBN: 978-1-941830-51-2 (digital)

Library of Congress Control Number: 2016953164

To Elliot,
who has always seen the value in what I do,
whether it be making sculptures, painting, or teaching;
who encouraged me to write the women's stories;
who has loved me selflessly and completely since we were teenagers.
I am forever grateful I get to share my life with you.

To Ty and Kaia, my beautiful children,
who help me see myself through their loving eyes;
who believe in me, no matter what;
who amaze me with their insights and compassion;
who light the world with their kindness and caring.
From the first moment I saw each of you,
I knew something deeper and more profound than even love.

Contents

Fish jumping

Every day I walk the river. The C&O Canal runs on one side and the flowing Potomac on the other. I walk between them on the dirt towpath that stretches for miles, the trees and vines my compadres. It's heavenly, a welcome refuge from the busy, crowded life around Washington, D.C. It's natural and peaceful. In the warm weather the turtles stretch out and sun themselves on logs. My dog Wiley and I often see herons, kingfishers, hawks, the vividly patterned wood ducks. Snakes. Occasionally we've seen beavers, and on one glorious day, a red fox in the glittering white snow.

One day as we walked, I heard a splash. Out of the corner of my eye I saw a fish jump out of the canal. As I stopped to look, she jumped again, and then again. By the third leap I could make out her head, fins, tail — her whole body. I had forgotten there even were fish in these waters.

That's what I think it's like for many of us. We travel through hectic days gliding on the surface of our lives, unaware of the vast treasures quietly waiting below.

I believe that by using our innate natural instincts we can reach beneath the surface, below that everyday veneer, and access the fertile world of our creativity.

Art is a portal. Through it we can explore these mysterious

depths, see the beauty of our world more clearly, understand ourselves and others more deeply, and realize the gift of our individuality. Like walks along the river, making art is a journey of illumination and possibility, pregnant with potential for ourselves, those we touch, and ultimately, beyond.

A fog is on the river. Everything looks a little unreal as I gaze into the nothingness. The path is strewn with iridescent yellow, red, and green leaves. I walk amongst them like a queen. The smell — pure autumn. In a few days the leaves will be tattered and brown. On our return the mist has disappeared. The red and yellow trees across the river are now crystal clear. Later the warm morning light will dim as the afternoon clouds cover my clear blue sky. In just a month or so, the bare trees will be white with snow.

RIVER LESSON: *Always, change*

THE BEGINNING

When we make art, we use our eyes and hands. Also, our bodies, our minds, our hearts, our souls. Creating art is an intellectual, psychological, physiological, and spiritual pursuit. We use our senses, even some yet to be named. When engaged in the act of making art, myriad components of our entire being are discharging simultaneously. It is enthralling and compelling. Thrilling. Exhilarating. Sometimes, calming. A complex and unique experience, unlike any other.

I've loved making art since I was a little girl. When I was really young, the boys on our dead-end street would play ball while I sat happily on the curb, mixing dirt and water into mudpies. At school, the margins of my notebooks were crowded with sketches: my preferred way to escape while sitting in class. At home I'd spend hours working on a drawing, enthralled by the way the soft stick of charcoal expressed the emotion I wanted in my work. Art transported me to a mystical world that was free and brilliant and inspiring.

I was seventeen when I started teaching, thrilled to head Arts & Crafts at my beloved sleep-away camp in the Pocono Mountains, elated to be creating and teaching art all day every day. In the ensuing twenty or so years I had the privilege of sharing my love of art with four-year-olds through high-school seniors on both sides of the country. For all of them, my avid hope was to nurture the joys of art making and to proffer creativity as a path for observing and responding to our world and ourselves.

Some years back, I left the San Francisco Bay area and my job teaching art at a prominent private school. I landed in the suburbs of Washington, D.C. After a few years of painting, drawing, and raising my children, I considered my job options. It was a regular discussion with my dear friend, Judy Segal. Back and forth we tossed around what work might interest me. One thing I knew for sure was that I didn't want to stray from art. Other friends had long suggested that I teach adults, but I wasn't convinced. I didn't want to teach painting or drawing; there were already very capable people doing that.

Then one day, after a series of emails back and forth, Judy wrote, "I think you should teach a class called Releasing the Creative Powers Within." The idea resonated instantly. I could see it: I would create a safe, nurturing space where creativity could flow unfettered. Authority would be in the hands of the student; I would be less a teacher and more of a trailblazer, gently guiding and pointing out the cool sights along the river of creative endeavors, sharing methods to access and express whatever was found along the way. Now this was something I could get into.

The class would be for women only, to allow for the greatest degree of comfort. I would work alongside them, modeling the process. If they needed help or advice I could easily stop what I was doing to guide them back on course. Technique would come, but on an as-needed basis. Steering the boat would be their personal vision. Experiential learning, driven by desire.

I would show the students works by historic and current artists to provide inspiration and reassurance that it was indeed worthwhile to create. I would use music, poetry, nature, writing, and jumping-off points to help them find their way in. An atmosphere of acceptance and compassion would allow and encourage voices within to rise up and release in the form of artistic expression.

A few months after Judy's prescient email, I opened up my studio to my first class of six women. The title: *Releasing the Creative Powers Within.*

When I opened my doors, I knew what I'd be bringing: a lifetime of guiding others in the making of art, a supreme regard for the spirit of creativity, a strong belief in every person's right to self-expression, and an abiding appreciation for the journey of self-discovery.

But I really had no clue what the women would bring. Though I am one myself, I had no idea of the depth and kindness of women. Moreover, I did not anticipate the profound transformative shifts these classes would spur in their lives, or the truths they would unearth and share.

Since that first day, scores of amazing women have taken seats around my studio table. They've included lawyers and psychotherapists, a practicing anesthesiologist, yoga instructors, a newspaper columnist, school teachers, a dental hygienist, poets, a nurse practitioner, life coaches, a financial analyst, realtors, a childcare worker, an architect, a congressional lobbyist, and on and on. Some were mothers with children still at home, some had children grown and out of the house, and some were young and single. I've had classes with a fifty-year age span in a single group of twelve women.

In the pages that follow, I describe my philosophy of creativity. I share *river lessons*: thoughts on nature and life garnered from my walks by the Potomac.

And I tell the women's stories. I describe how creating a womb-like vessel allowed Faith to grieve for a baby miscarried years before; how Jess' exploration of fear let her come to terms with abuse suffered as a child; how Kim turned a handful of clay into a powerful talisman that helped her cope with her teenage son's cancer.

I quote the women as they reflect on their lives and their art, and as they uncover inner complexities, discover core beliefs, rid themselves of unproductive patterns, find new truths, and forge new paths. Through their stories and the accompanying photographs, you'll see how art has awakened, enriched, and deepened their lives. Creativity holds profound treasures for every one of us, and that is the ultimate message I hope you will take from this book.

The portraits and stories that follow are true. The names have been changed for the sake of privacy. I thank each of these women for their openness and generosity in allowing me to share their stories.

Wiley and I are stretched out on our favorite rock. The river, just below, roars as the water whirls by. I close my eyes to hear. The call of a crow. A pileated woodpecker tap-tap-tapping on a tree. The mating songs of the cicadas growing louder and louder and then quieting down again. I blink my eyes open to a half dozen goslings gliding in a line.

RIVER LESSON: *Follow your instincts*

Art is our birthright

It's a desire. A yearning. For some, it's a need. To express ourselves. To make a mark. We are drawn to create something where there was nothing. Consider young children and their boundless delight as they color or play with clay. Or hammer wood. This is where we all begin. Creativity comes to us instinctively. It is our birthright.

Long ago art was intertwined with everyday life. Our ancestors coiled the clay bowls they cooked in, sewed the clothes they wore, hammered their own tools. And when they made their pots they didn't stop at making them functional, they designed them to be unique and beautiful. They dyed flax to make their clothing colorful. Art and life entwined. We know that people have been drawing and painting at least since we lived in caves; we are so fortunate to still have the exquisite cave paintings they were moved to make. This is our heritage, the legacy of each and every one of us. As long as there have been people, in all corners of the earth, we have been making art. It is a natural, primal facet of being human.

During my years working with children, many parents furtively shared with me a sense of remorse for the loss of creativity in their own lives. Some recalled a precipitating incident that ruined it for them: the harsh judgments of a teacher, expectations they felt unable to fulfill, or just a natural stumbling point in their art with no one to help carry them over. But, to a person, they felt the loss and wished to have the wondrous sense of creating back in their lives again. They envied their children.

I believe this loss is even more profound than many of us realize. These adults, and so many others, have lost not only the wonder of their own creativity, but much more, because, through art:

- We can express ourselves in ways that words cannot. Making art is a unique mode of expression like no other.

- We can see our world more deeply. When we draw, we see in a way that is so clear, so attuned, that we get to see unheralded beauty even in the commonplace.

- We can view the creativity of others with newfound appreciation and enjoyment.

- We can discover thoughts and feelings we never knew we had, learning about ourselves and others along the way.

- We can enjoy the feel of a soft pastel as it warms the paper, our body and chalk moving in tandem, as we dance with the muse.

In adulthood, when making art ceases to be *child's* play, a kind of elite status emerges, an unspoken conviction that if you are not a professional artist you have no real right to make art. Either you have talent or you don't, and if you don't, then don't bother. People buy into this theft of their birthright, relying on the oft-repeated refrain: "I can't even draw a straight line." Well, since when was drawing a straight line a prerequisite for sketching? We have rulers for that. There are many kinds of media for the making of art and endless ways of being creative. Drawing is just one.

Tell me, why is there this exclusionary distinction between art and the rest of life's great pleasures? If you're not born a virtuoso pianist, do you not still learn to play the piano? And do you not still enjoy it? It's gratifying, even if you're not a prodigy, even if you don't have a special talent. Even though you're not Tiger Woods, do you not still enjoy swinging a golf club? Why should art be any different? We can each learn to improve and progress, to become a more proficient draughtsman if that's what we want, or more skilled at throwing a pot on the potter's wheel, or we can learn to weld metal or blow glass. But no matter the medium, or the mode, it's ours for the taking. For the freedom. For what we might learn about ourselves. For possibility's sake. For the sheer joy of it!

Today the water is high and muddy, gushing from the series of storms we've had the last couple of days. Wiley and I sit on our rock. Glittering in the murky water below are dozens of fish struggling to swim upstream. In the span of a half hour, I watch hundreds of them force their way beside the rocks, through the rush of the channel. Some are driven back, but turn around to try again. Just beyond there is a little inlet, water calm and smooth. Once there, the fish dwell a while, resting from their labors.

RIVER LESSON: *Struggle reaps reward*

Day 1

When I began the classes, my idea was to offer an inspiring, supportive place for women, a respite from their busy, caretaking days. I wanted to offer my students the opportunity to rediscover their creativity and open doors of possibility. I hoped to help them let go, to give them time when they could just be, and more than anything, I hoped to give them a place where they could feel free.

I wasn't sure who would come, whether women would be open to the experience, or what they'd think. This was Bethesda, a suburb of Washington, after all. Here, in the D.C. area, people can be so conservative. Would anyone take the chance and "come to some stranger's home for hours," as one of my students once quipped, to a class called *Releasing the Creative Powers Within?* I didn't know if I could even get one class of six women together. But they came. In fact, the class filled up so quickly that I offered a second section before I even started teaching the first. It seemed that women were hungry for something. So, I had two classes of six women each and I was ready to go. I was thinking I wouldn't do things a whole lot differently from when I worked with children: teach with respect and enthusiasm for the women's creative impulses.

But on the very first day of the very first class, I realized that this would be different from all my prior years of teaching. I told the women a bit about myself and my hopes for the class. I let them know that my studio was a sacred space, that almost no one had ever been allowed in there. Until then. I advised them that no inner critics would be permitted in the space; we would let them sail away through the windows. I told them that this time and this work was just for them, that there would be an opportunity to share their work and their process, but it would be absolutely voluntary to allow for total freedom and openness.

Then, almost in passing, I asked what brought them to the class. I expected they would say they wanted to learn how to make art, unleash their creativity — quick, perfunctory answers. But instead there was an outpouring. And that's when I began to grasp what we were opening up. The women began to speak about families who depended on them, demanding jobs, sick kids: the strains and pulls of women's lives.

They explained that these couple of hours they'd set aside for themselves were rare and precious ones. Gina said, "I've spent the last couple of years hospicing three relatives — my father, my grandmother, and my aunt — and now I need to take care of myself." Julia talked about the loss of her very closest friend who had passed away just a couple of months before, and her hope to do some artwork around that loss. Another told us how, though her mother was an artist, as a child she had been scolded for using her mother's art supplies and working "the wrong way." I suddenly realized: this is going to be very different from what I'd foreseen. This is going to be intense. Deep. And very, very meaningful.

It's been a long, chilly winter. Trudging the icy path, I eagerly anticipate the beautiful rapture of spring. But day after day, the forest branches are bare, the ground cold and hard. Today, though, the path is almost clear, and finally I see the sweet green of baby leaves. Suddenly spring is everywhere. A quickening underground has come to pass. And now, springtime shines in the light of day.

RIVER LESSON: *Change comes in quiet*

Lighting the Way

Well it's like this: I set the scene; music is integral. I play music of a similar mood throughout. It quietly occupies the thinking brain so the deep and profound soul can come forward. But first . . . first I want everyone to feel comfortable. I serve them tea, coffee. They're in my home. There's a natural warmth from the light coming in the studio windows. I'm looking to evoke a mood and, over time, a kind of post-hypnotic suggestion of being here, feeling open and free.

Often, near the start of class, we stop for a few moments to make the transition from the hectic outside world to the quiet, internal realm of art making. We write. It slows us down, brings us into the present. We might take a few moments to breathe, to look and listen inward. Sometimes I lead a guided meditation. In order to hear our soft inner voice, we need quiet and calm. You can feel the settling as it fills the room. The release in sighs is telling.

A doctor in the group, tips of her fingers touching her wrist, says, "My pulse slows just being here." With the pace slowed and bodies relaxed, the women are able to reflect on what is truly important to them. As one student wrote me: "I am looking forward to what I regard as my peaceful island in the whirring world around me!" The class is safe harbor.

But even in the safety of the studio, there are concerns. There's doubt among the women that their work won't measure up. They express apprehension that they work too slowly (or too quickly); that their own work is transparent while that of others is mysterious; that theirs is too symbolic . . . or not symbolic enough.

Comparison to others and relentless self-judgment hold us back, keeping us from being fully ourselves. Withholding self-acceptance keeps us from fulfilling who we are and what we have to give. It keeps us down. When we compare ourselves to others, we give our power away.

I do everything I can think of to help everyone feel at ease, yet the truth is that this is a venture into the unknown. There are worries: Will I really be able to make art? How will these people view my work? How will the other women judge me? What secrets will my work betray? And ultimately: How will I see myself? Will I measure up?

These are valid concerns. To delve into our deeper selves necessitates vulnerability — especially in a group setting — and that can be scary. But unless we are willing to be open, only the superficial will show itself.

When Jan first joins the class her disquiet is palpable. Yet, as she gets drawn into the colors, the soft touch of the clay, and the lull of the music, she feels the other women's calm and the comfort of the space. I quietly watch as she begins to leave her fears behind. She lets her heart be her guide, and her inner critic is left to the sidelines. Integrating herself into the process, truth begins to materialize in her hands. As they warm and soften the clay, who is better or faster or slower becomes insignificant. The import becomes the work and her connection with it. There is a transformation as she and the clay become one. Time is irrelevant: Jan is in the work, in the river of creativity.

When done, Jan surfaces, and looks around to see what she and others in the class have created. One thing she cannot help but notice is the distinctiveness of each and every piece. Given the very same materials and topic, each woman's piece is unlike every other. The inimitability of the work is amazing, powerful, inspiring. It is clear: we each bring a unique expression to the work and hence, to the group. No one could have made Jan's piece and she could have made no one else's. This insight is revelatory, not only for the work at hand, but for the deeper implications about herself and every one of us. It is inescapable: each piece, and therefore each of us, is divinely and perfectly unique.

With this awareness ultimately comes appreciation, and the solid truth that the more we embrace our uniqueness, the more we accept ourselves as we are, the more we realize what we alone have to give. This is a powerful truth to carry into the world. For as we appreciate and value our own uniqueness, so will we value that of others. And in so doing, a ripple of awareness, acceptance, and gratitude is set in motion. With gratitude comes love, with love comes compassion. And compassion is what we need more of in this world.

On the way to our rock there's a parting of the trees. Wiley and I stop to take in the view. Way beyond where we stand, far as the eye can see, the river turns. It feels like an opening. I breathe it in.

RIVER LESSON: *Openings reveal possibility*

Openings

Sometimes, when we open a part of ourselves that has been blocked or underused for a long time, other parts of ourselves spontaneously unlock in a kind of unconscious restructuring. I've seen this awe-inspiring phenomenon many times. Creating, in a very deep and personal way, unleashes a concurrent energy that gently blows open doors within one's self and in one's life. The opening is a mysterious thoroughfare. I think I love the opening itself as much as I love what waits on the other side.

The women talk about it. Sometimes the process of opening up brings revelation. A woman may now see herself or the world with new clarity or compassion, or she may discover a new sense of self. "The other day at work," Jo told us, "I stood up for myself like I never have before. I was totally shocked! I thought, 'Where the heck did that come from?' But I knew instantly: Art Class!"

Sometimes it's about seeing the world through fresh eyes: "I'm so much more aware of colors, patterns, and shapes. I'm seeing the world in whole new ways."

Often, the openings allow for a greater appreciation of artwork that had before seemed incomprehensible. "I am now open to appreciating modern art! I went to the Museum of Modern Art today and I totally enjoyed all the surprising, sometimes bewildering artwork. I just allowed myself to be moved."

It happens in so many different ways. Sometimes our children notice a newfound sense of fun and exploration in their moms, and the kids begin to make more art themselves. "When I bring home a creation from art class my children and their friends are really intrigued and excited. They all want to try it, and we do!" And so the women pass the joys of creativity along to the next generation.

Life changes are made. More than once, the opening has revealed a career that had been buried in a pile of uncertainty. After returning to school for her master's degree in Decorative Arts of the Twentieth Century, Sally wrote, "Believe it or not I never would have done it without art class!"

Bea, a banker by profession, credits her time in the class with her decision to sell her house near Washington, D.C. and move to her dream home in the country. "Art class helped me realize what's really important. I have always wished for a slower way of life but it's been subjugated to everything else," says Bea. "Now, I get to watch horses from my living room window every day!"

The opening for Annie came quite literally through her artwork, unbeknownst even to her.

Annie entered her first class as a quiet and thoughtful seventy-five-year-old who had lost her husband the previous year. She had shuttered herself away since, buried in grief. She came into my studio and spoke of how, after all the tears, she was looking to renew her life. I was glad that our first project centered around the idea of life as a journey.

While Annie and the other women might be quite accomplished in other areas of their lives, many of them are completely new to art making. They may be afraid or unsure of where to begin. Jumping-off points help the women find their way into a project, giving them something to lean on, a place to begin. I really love the Life as a Journey jumping-off point. It connotes time and movement, but nary a destination. Instead of having to be somewhere, the voyage itself is all. I thought it would suit Annie well at this turning point in her life.

To begin, Annie took a few moments to write, transitioning from the rush of the morning to the calm of the studio, getting in touch with her quiet voice within. Pondering the idea of life as a journey, she wrote about the roles she'd had — daughter, sister, wife, friend, mother . . . . She wrote about where she'd been, where she was headed, where she might like to be going.

Once she'd written, she could let the thoughts go. She didn't need to hold them in her head; the left-brain work was done. Now it was time to release preconceived notions and allow the materials to lead. Assorted hues of soft clay, wooden tools and rolling pins were within her reach in the center of the work area. Annie closed her journal. She chose some muted colors and began to work the clay. Slowly but surely a thick coil began to stretch and mold into an archway. After getting the arch to stand tall, she took her castoff clay and dreamily formed small balls in the palms of her hands. As I watched from the corner of my eye, she lightly tossed the balls through the arch.

When her artwork felt complete she wrote about how it felt to work with clay and about the piece itself, how it evolved, about whatever came. This post-creating writing can be enlightening; it's not every day we stop and consider our lives as journeys. And it's more rare still to work without thinking, being led instead by our deep inner guide.

When it came Annie's opportunity to talk about the experience, she offhandedly shared that she spent a great deal of time with her grandchildren, and so she had made a kind of game. She said no more about it.

But I suspected something else. I saw an opening that she herself could pass through. Her archway felt to me like a beginning.

The next week Annie returned to class with a changed persona. She was glowing with excitement and could hardly wait to tell us what had transpired since we all last met.

She began by explaining that in the year since her beloved husband passed away, she had been too brokenhearted to use her kitchen. She'd made easy meals, like hamburgers and sandwiches, but nothing more involved. "You see", she said softly, "the kitchen had always been the center of our family's life — my husband and me, our children, our grandchildren — the place where we always gathered. There were so many memories in that kitchen — it was just too painful." But last week, "I was kind of impulsively stopping at markets and buying ingredients — herbs, rice, pasta — without really thinking. And then, on Saturday night, I found myself barefoot and in the kitchen, cooking up a storm into the wee hours of the morning! I was making white rice, brown rice, bulgur, macaroni and cheese, a new recipe for chicken — concoctions I've never in my life tried before," she laughed. Annie had cooked up a celebratory feast. "In the morning I called my children and invited them all over for Sunday dinner. When they saw all the foods I'd prepared, they were in shock. It was the best evening I've had in a very long time. I believe that, somehow, the work I did in class has allowed me to start living again."

Beautiful rain-soaked day. The trail is wet with puddles. Something is glinting, eye level. A tiny apple-green inchworm is hanging over the trail in mid-air. It seems like she's floating, the minute thread she's hanging by invisible to my naked eye. I glance up to see where she's coming from. I look up higher, and higher still. This little inchworm has made her way down from a tree limb that must be eighty feet high, lowering herself inch by inch to the forest floor.

RIVER LESSON: *Patience*

Writing

I ask the women to write at least once a day, even when they're not in class. It doesn't have to be a lot of writing—just to touch pen to paper is enough. If there is more to say, it will come.

We write in class as well, integrating our reflections into our artistic endeavors. Writing before starting a project gives voice to unfocused thoughts and emotion, shedding light in some hazy corners. Writing after completing a piece enlightens uniquely. In myriad ways, writing rounds out and adds to our comprehension of our work and our selves.

When creating artwork intuitively, from deep inner resources instead of our routine thought modes, our thinking mind reflexively generates explanations about the meaning of a piece as we go. But while these seeming elucidations that float through our minds as our hands create may make conscious sense and may tell part of the story, they don't reach the profound truths emanating from deep within. We could leave it there; these products of our always-thinking minds do work as explanations. But by investigating the work through the act of writing afterward, we attain an unparalleled entrée into the deeper realms of the unconscious and into deeper levels of realization. I have seen this confirmed over and over again, often with surprising revelations. Exactly how it works is a mystery to me, but time and time again, writing sheds new light.

I'd often witnessed this phenomenon when hearing the women talk about their deep cognitions through writing, but its resounding significance became undeniable for me with an experience of my own.

We were doing a project around the notion of caretakers. The idea of a guardian angel was in the back of my mind when I created my two cloth figures: a white winged angel holding a smaller childlike figure wrapped in a silken multi-colored cloak (right).

When it came time for sharing I hadn't yet had a chance to write about my piece. That was fine with me, because I knew what it was about. I went ahead and shared my thoughts about the two characters I had created. It was obvious to me, as I shared with the class, that the angel was a beautiful, loving guardian and the small figure was me, in child mode. My child within was being held and protected by this comforting, soft angel. The explanation seemed obvious and right and that was that.

But the following day, in the next class, I had the opportunity to write about the pieces before sharing again. (A bonus of teaching the classes: I get to take them all.) As soon as the words, "what my figures are about" flowed from my pen, a realization blew through me. One figure was not an angel and the other me. The truth — the greater truth — was that the two

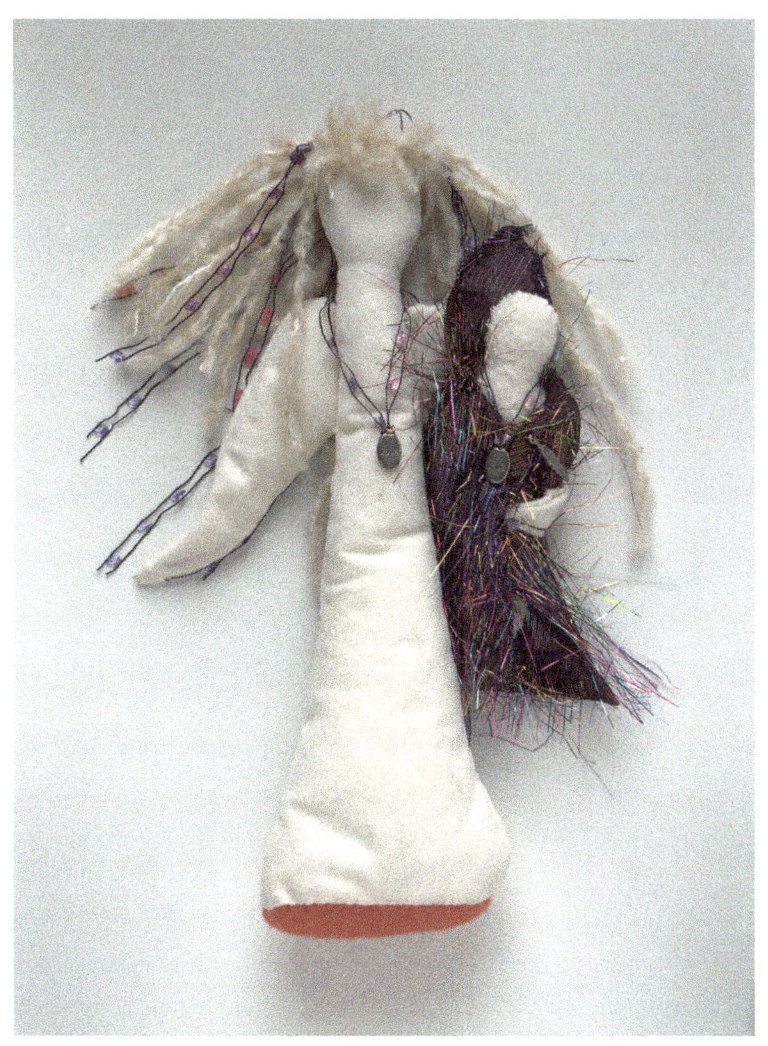

figures were me: angel and child both. This revelation — that I was and have always been my own loving guardian angel — was a striking epiphany for me, one that I continue to cherish. It was an awareness I believe I never would have been privy to, had I not written. It took the act of putting pen to paper. There is just something revelatory about that act.

As soon as the realization emerged, it crystallized, becoming even more clear, and obvious, really. Indeed, I'd given both angel and child identical necklaces. And I'd trimmed the pure white angel with a soft red cloth, which I now understood represented her foundation; red had come to symbolize my personal foundation in much of my work over the previous months. But I hadn't put it all together, until I wrote.

From this experience I saw more clearly than ever the power of writing as a valuable and inexorable facet of our work.

For adults who haven't made art since childhood, returning to their creativity can be very freeing. We have a child within us still, and she still loves colors, the spontaneity of play, the surprise of seeing something new and unanticipated appear. As one student said, "I feel like I've encountered a girl who has slept for a long time inside me."

When making art in an authentic way, beautiful pieces naturally emerge, as truth is beauty. Sometimes unexpected insights occur, and writing expands upon them exponentially.

Gina, a poet, chose to use one of her poems as a launch for a piece in clay. She reflected on her poem and let the clay tell her story, creating a dynamic and perceptibly deep work: tall and undulating grey walls surrounded a flat red spiral in the center. On the spiral lay a long red eel with sharp points poking out of it.

Gina felt she had a pretty good handle on what her piece was about, sharing with the class the work's connection to her childhood and her difficult relationship with her father. "My father had huge parts of his life completely walled off from us. I guess that's what the wall is about."

The following week Gina came back, eager to elaborate upon what she had shared earlier: "I had the piece sitting in the seat beside me when I drove home from class last week. At a stoplight it caught my eye and I had a sudden flash of insight. I had to stop the car. I pulled over, and wrote and wrote and wrote. The words just poured out of me. And, as they did, the piece revealed more and more, like I was peeling away the layers of an onion. It's true that it was about my father, but there was so much more to it. I was in the piece too, which earlier I hadn't realized at all. And I finally found an undeniable sense of forgiveness towards my father that I have never in my life felt before."

Walking the trail one bright spring morning, I glance across the canal to the sloping woods on the other side. Something in the tall grass catches my eye. I focus, and make out a young doe lying there, peering at me through the grass. Entrancing. Never before have I seen a deer resting in the woods. Usually they're on the move, foraging or walking, or on the run, their white tails high in the air. In the past I've found impressions of where they'd slept, but never before have I seen one in her cozy nest, gazing back at me.

RIVER LESSON: *Discoveries await*

Discoveries

Early on in one of the classes we did a doll project. I say "doll" in the loosest sense of the word; they were actually artworks fabricated from cloth and stuffing. Any shape, any size, notes hidden within, charms dangling, bells, feathers . . . .

And the jumping-off point I offered students to consider: If you had a protector, what would he or she be? What would she do for you? Would she shelter you from others? Protect you from the ways in which you hurt yourself? What would she look like? Would she build a wall around you? Or help you take your walls down?

The women wrote, then chose fabrics and materials that spoke to them and their visions . . . and set to work.

I love the dolls they created. Some were fun, some were elegant, some outlandish, some were heartfelt images of themselves or their wished-for protectors. Some were cozy, to snuggle with in bed, while others spoke for them, through them.

It was Gwen's first time taking the class. She had always yearned to make art but sorely doubted her abilities. Gwen is full of life. She thinks fast, moves fast, talks fast, and works fast — a quick and competent woman. She was edgy about the slow, repetitive process of sewing by hand, and worried that she wouldn't come up with anything that had real meaning for her. Pressing on, she chose plain white muslin and started piecing together a simple shape, similar to the example I'd made for the class. She hesitantly began her stitching, shaky about how to proceed, and dubious that she would be pleased with anything she'd create.

At the end of the class, Gwen took her just-started doll home. Late that night, she was drawn to take up her doll again. As she stitched, she continued to question whether she could even do the project; it felt so contrived. Still, she finished the initial shape and began to sew on some charms, at first planning it out: "this heart is for my daughter," "this charm represents my mom," "this charm represents my love for my husband," but then the charms started to go on without a plan, without any thought. She began to be one with her piece, in the moment, and her inner judge was finally quiet.

She confided to us in the next class: "As I wove the needle in and out of my fabric, an image of my husband came to me. I'd been thinking about how I'm always pulling him along, trying to get him to keep up with me. It's like I'm speeding along, and he's forever lagging behind. I'm looking back, imploring him to keep up. But as I stitched, a realization rose up. It shook me to the core: My husband has not been behind me — not at all. On the contrary — he has been right beside me all the way, supporting my every step." This sudden revelation of her husband and their relationship stunned, and then elated her.

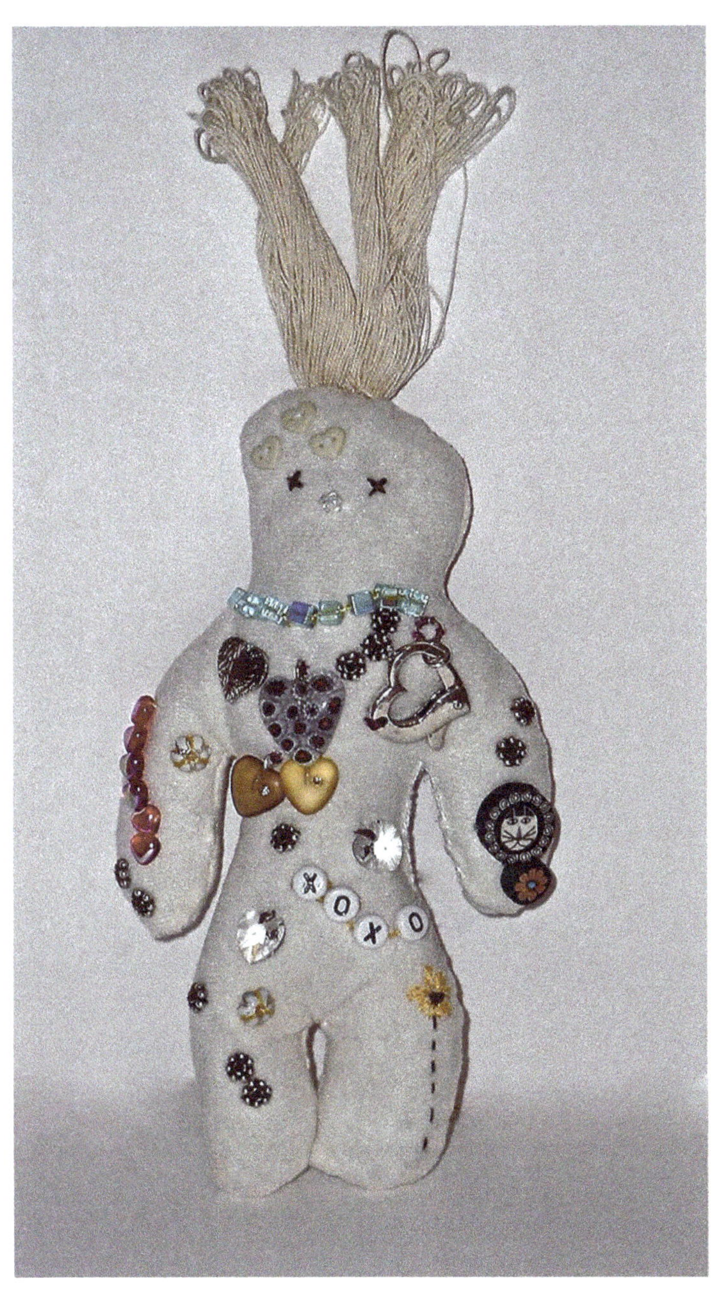

Months later Gwen reflected, "That single thought has become a core belief in my marriage, and I treasure it. Those kind of thoughts don't come easily. And I love my doll. She sits on a little leather turquoise cufflink box in my favorite spot in my house."

The joy is palpable in Gwen's piece (page 59).

How does this profound kind of change and revelation come to be? By quieting down our usual patterns of thought and by letting go of our inner critic. By being willing. By feeling safe. By becoming open to what may come. There are truths within us. With openness, our truths emerge and change our lives.

Grace is one of the most even-keeled people I have ever known, and I know her well. She has taken my classes for years, and she's a close friend and neighbor. She's bright and thoughtful, a wife and mother, and a practicing anesthesiologist. She has one day off during her busy workweek and saves the morning for her Thursday art class. She will gladly tell you how much she has learned both about herself and about making art over the years, but the fabric doll project surprised and delighted her more profoundly than all the others.

Actually, Grace didn't just create a doll. She created an entire scene. As she worked, I could sense her satisfaction from across the studio.

Her piece (right) looked like this: On a soft ground of moss and flowers stood a stuffed tree that Grace had sewn in a deep brown fabric. In the corner where limb and trunk meet perched

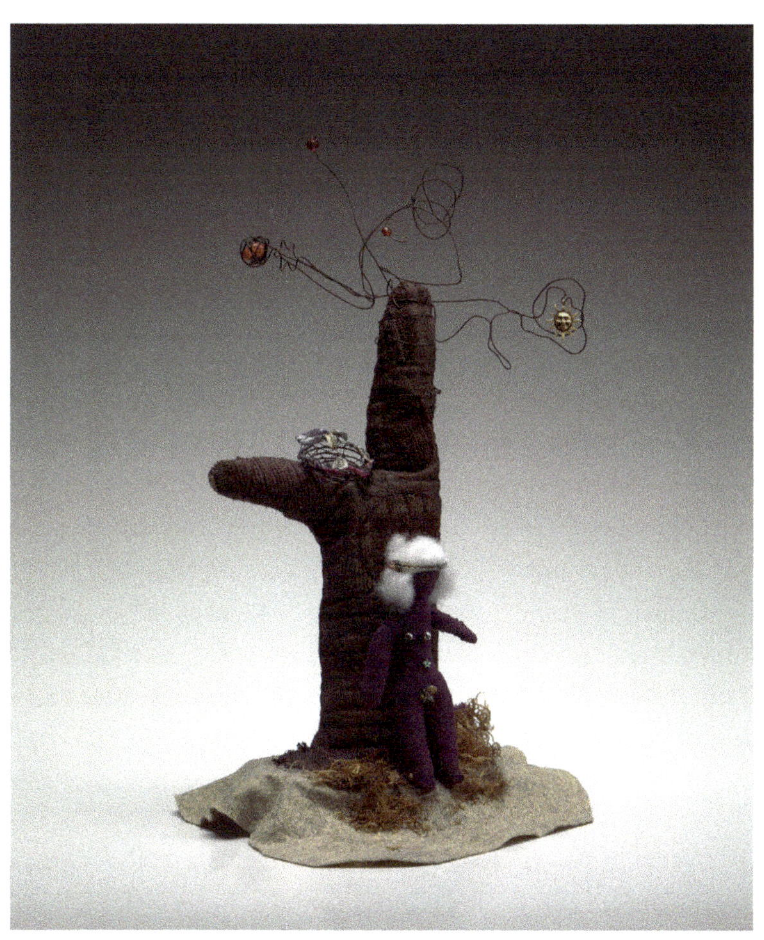

a small, well protected nest. Spiraling out from the treetop was flowing copper wire, with curling ends encasing stones and charms.

Against the tall tree trunk stood a cloth, three-dimensional woman. She too was sewn by hand and stuffed, and her color was deep violet. She was unclothed. Touches of bells and charms defined her private parts. But, by far, the most eye-catching aspect of this woman was her shock of wild white hair and the bandanna tied around her head, 1960s style.

Grace was pleased. She excitedly told us that it was the first time, in all her classes here, that the piece itself guided her. She let it lead. "I just followed."

This was clearly a significant piece for Grace, in part for her newfound process, and in part for the enthralling depth of meaning so surely conveyed in the work. She mused about the piece with the class, pondered it's meaning. She shared that it felt to her like the piece had something to do with strength, but she didn't have much more of a clue than that.

My feeling was that the piece was not made by her mind and was not really accessible through it. This piece was made from heart and soul, and that was where the answers were to be found. It was the woman against the tree who most interested me. I've known Grace for years, and I was struck that this woman didn't seem like her. Our artwork is a reflection of ourselves. But it didn't seem to be the case here. I was baffled by the cloth woman and by where Grace was to be found in her very personal piece.

I asked her about the woman as she finished up her sharing. Grace smiled at me, "I don't know, I really don't know who she is. I'm very curious about her." Then she asked me if I knew, with that look on her face that intimated: "You know something, don't you?"

"No, I have no idea," I answered. And I didn't.

Since Grace was so intrigued about the piece's deeper significance, I suggested that she write about it. Actually, not so much that she write about the piece, really, but more that she write to the piece, and ask the woman directly who she was. It may sound crazy, but sometimes when we write to our work, or elements of it, and ask our questions, answers come, maybe from deep down inside ourselves, but they come.

A few days later Grace phoned me, energized. She had found her answer. "This morning I was running on the treadmill, and my piece was on a table in front of me. I decided to ask the woman who she was. I was in a state of openness and felt ready for a response. As soon as I asked, the woman turned to me. And I could see her face. She's my mother."

Grace went into more depth with her classmates. "I suddenly remembered that one day, when I was a teenager, my mother came home with her hair in a full Afro. She was so happy. She was just beaming. I remember that day with great fondness." Grace said that after her revelation, "I ran to my photos and found a picture of my mother from that time, from that moment, actually. It has the exact feel of the figure in my piece."

Grace had decided she wanted to give the piece to her mother as a gift, but for some reason she wasn't feeling able to part with it. Something was holding her back. Time went by. One day, as she was looking at the piece, a second revelation emerged. It suddenly became clear that the tree upon which her mother leaned was none other than Grace herself. Ahh, and there it was. Grace was the tree supporting her mother, and the strength she had mentioned in her initial sharing. With the clarity she gained from her reflections, she was able to give the piece, without reservation, to her mother.

Grace later told me, "That piece was, for me, tremendously moving, because it demonstrated maturity, understanding, and forgiveness. And, when I gave that piece to my mother for her seventieth birthday, it was absolutely a new beginning for us."

There's a huge old tree slumped across the path today. She must have crashed during the high winds last night. I remember her from when she stood. Magnificent — huge, weighty branches reaching out and up. I admired her majesty. But — she was rotted, empty inside. I can see that now.

RIVER LESSON: *Without support we cannot stand*

Facing Fear

We live in reality. Or we think we do, anyway. But reality is forever entwined with our perceptions, the tint of the glasses through which we view the world, even how we perceive our very selves. Our *glasses* are colored by many things, both seen and unseen, some from the past, some from the present, and some from anticipating our future.

Many of our perspectives are valid and useful. But others are tinged by experiences and worries from long ago, remnants woven so deeply within that we may not even recognize what they have come to be: habituated patterns of thought and feelings that distort the truth. Ideas that may have, at an earlier time, been useful coping systems, but have since morphed into roadblocks, keeping us from fulfilling the potential of our lives. They may reflect the tint of who we believe we are, but shortchange the full spectrum of who we can truly be.

A friend of mine travels all over the country helping people sort out social and psychological issues in their lives and businesses. Of all the obstacles they face, Robert says, "the biggest thing that holds people back and thwarts their potential is fear. It's the biggie."

Fear is big. A necessary and useful emotion, it keeps us aware and safe, but fear can also dominate our minds pointlessly. We've all had fears that we know are irrational and even harmful, but they can be hard to control. Fear can become inflated and overwhelming, ruling our lives toward no real worthwhile end. It can keep us from moving forward, restrict us from reaching our potential and our happiness.

As I walked the river one cold and windy morning, I considered using fear as a jumping-off point. It would surely be worthwhile; I mean, how can one *release their creative powers within* if fear is in the way? And yet I had hesitations: fear and anxiety is a foreboding realm, one we don't venture into eagerly. Maybe the women wouldn't want to hazard there. Maybe I was taking the classes too far. But, knowing its domination over so much of our lives, even in seemingly small ways, I could no longer resist tackling the subject. Once I made the decision, I considered how to best set up a project. My steps quickened as I contemplated media and how to introduce the subject matter.

Fear can be insidious, with rationalizations only too happy to lend disguise. It is a shapeshifter, appearing one way in some situations, differently in others. The first step in confronting fear is to become aware of when it is leading us. So I asked the women to spend the week before starting the project noticing their fear, seeking it out, looking for where it was hiding.

On the day we began, I offered the women shallow, round pappier-mâché boxes measuring nine, eleven, or thirteen inches across. I chose these boxes very deliberately, searching until I found exactly what I wanted. It's crucial to have the apposite materials because they are the scaffolding on which a whole project rests. The right choice of media can make all the difference in facilitating surrender. Somehow, the size and shape of these sturdy boxes felt well suited for our work around fear, low-slung but with enough diameter to encompass some big truths. They had lids, allowing the option of containing whatever was inside, and were of a material that could be sliced into.

For a month we worked in the realm of fear. Writing about it, making art around it, pondering it, and sharing our thoughts. It was a very intense month.

I first met Jess when she came to the studio some eight years before. She hadn't done art since she was a kid, but something about my flier called to her. She loves to share with new students how she almost vomited on her ride over that first day, she was so terrified. And yet she came. And I've watched her and her work grow from tentative yearnings to an emboldened knowing. But her piece from the fear project is probably the most important she has done, as it brought her to unearth the most secreted-away incident of her life, allowing her to face it, share it, and move on.

Jess began by choosing one of the mid-sized boxes. She started painting, stroking layer after layer of color, and when she was done she had a very beautiful box: shades of rich golds, siennas, and purples. Soft and pretty, like Jess.

As she herself expressed it: "My box looked quite lovely. When I was done that first day I realized that what I had was

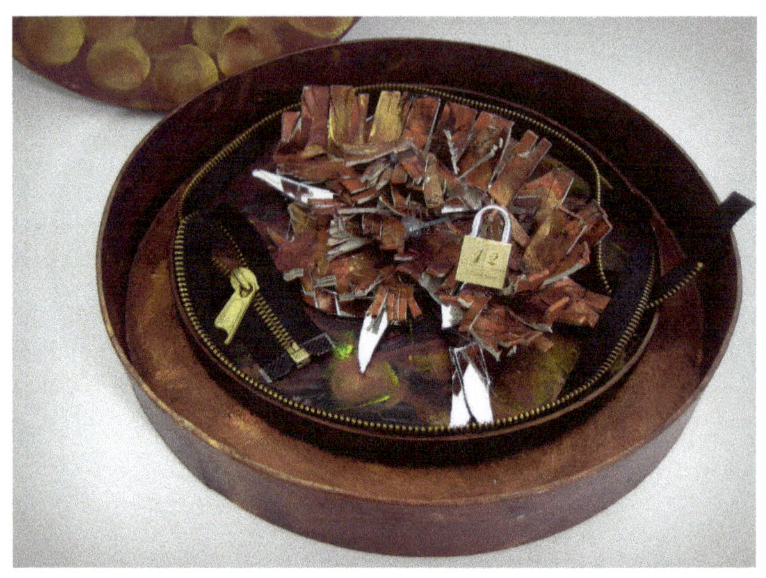

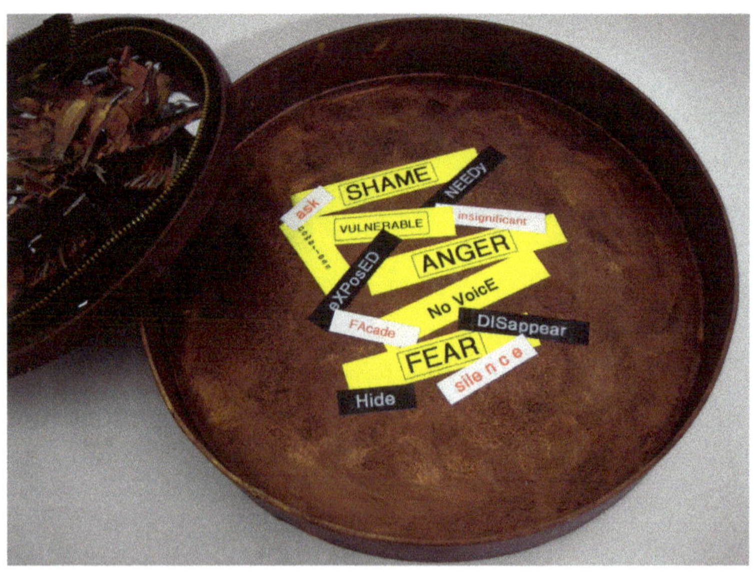
SHAME
NEEDy
ask
VULNERABLE
insignificant
ANGER
eXPosED
No VoicE
FAcade
DISappear
FEAR
sile n c e
Hide

a pretty, but empty, box. But the feeling was more about the empty."

She came into class the following week, chose a second, smaller box, and, again, out came the paints. Darker, heavier colors: reds and blacks. There were two boxes now, one inside the other. The two boxes didn't match or resemble each other. There was a beautiful box on the outside but the inner box was weighing it all down.

At home a couple of nights later, Jess was sitting, looking at the project when she was overcome with the feeling of wanting to cut up the dark box. "I took a knife to it and cut as hard and fast as I could," she said. "It felt like I was trying to make it disappear. I piled all the pieces up on a desk and just kept looking at them. It was very unnerving." The pieces had raw edges from being broken apart. She took the lid from the box she'd cut apart, placed it upside down in the bigger box, and piled all the jagged pieces into the middle.

Back in class, Jess added broken shards of mirror to the pile, but she left feeling very unsettled. Driving home, she had an overwhelming urge to stop at the five-and-dime to buy a zipper. "And when I put the zipper in there, that's when I knew what the project was about" (left, top).

One evening forty-five years earlier, Jess had gone to her father for guidance and support. "I was upset about a boy and was feeling vulnerable," she told me. "I went to my father asking for comfort and came away with sexual abuse. I was twelve years old. I made myself an unspoken rule that I would never, ever ask for anything again. I functioned that way for a very long time."

As Jess continued working on her piece, she glued words revealing the emotions she had kept to herself for so long (page 72, bottom). "ASK is the key word," she said, "because I went to my father that evening to ask something of him."

Other words were FEAR and ANGER. "The fear and anger that had been stuffed away for so long felt explosive and uncontrollable," Jess said. "The anger that rose up was what I was really afraid of. My own anger is my biggest fear. What would I do with that anger if I let it out?"

At the end of our private conversation, Jess said she wanted to share her reflections with her classmates. She was very close to the other women but was concerned about upsetting them. "What's inside this pretty box is a very dark place to take them."

Jess resolved to ask the women how they would feel about her sharing, letting them know her concerns. They reassured her that they wanted to support her and could handle whatever it was she had to say. She told them, "I want you to know that your thoughts are welcome, but it's also okay to say nothing at all. What I need is for you to be the observers, or witnesses. In the sharing and processing and being heard, I will be more grounded in myself."

Jess later told me, "I felt strong and cared for in the collective strength of the group. That was really very powerful for me. It's taken decades to see what happened, own it, observe it, and finally walk through it to the other side."

On the very top of Jess' box were little planters with overflowing moss (right). "This represents growth," she said, "and finally moving forward."

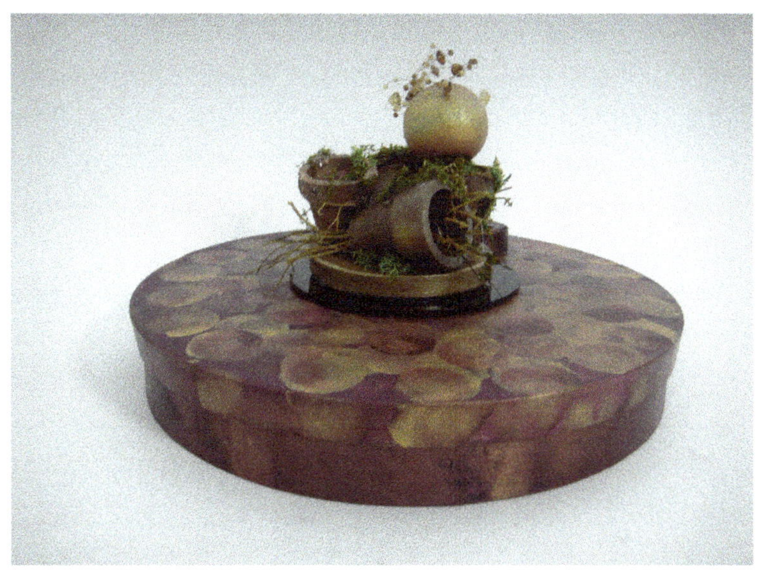

For my own project around fear, I chose one of the smaller nine-inch boxes, starting out, like many of us, by painting the container. I fiercely painted the inside of my box — red, black, yellow. Without deliberation, but with focused intensity, I just about pummeled in the colors. I slit a spiral inside the box with a mat knife, opening up a vortex in the bottom, like the bottomless pit fear can suck me down into. Steps led into the box, but not out. Broken jags of mirror shot up from the floor of the container and right out the lid. There was no containing this fear. It was a nasty mess, but it felt right. When Jess mentioned how she'd felt an entanglement of fear with anger in her own box, I too sensed the anger so obviously tied up with the fear in mine. In a common benefit of working in a group, her self-disclosure allowed me to see my own work more clearly.

I worked some more, adding a crazy maze of wire, banning any way out. More anger and fear and glue and mess piled up inside. This was my fear and my anger as I'd felt it millions of times. It was ugly and I was glad when class was over, and I could put the top of the box back on, or, as one of the women so aptly quipped, "put a lid on it." What a relief.

During the next class I knotted strands of taffeta around the perimeter of the box, urgently trying to contain the dreaded feelings inside. But I could see that wasn't right. I didn't want to just tamp the fear down, but I wasn't sure what to do with all that emotion.

The next morning I walked the river, mulling over fear, anger, and the intensity of my piece. In my contemplation I perceived humiliation. I suddenly grasped how my anger and fear were tied to humiliations suffered as a child, many years ago. And how, at times anyway, fear had been an age-old response to avoiding feeling that humiliation ever again. That avoidance, set up so many years ago, continued to rule my life. It was then that I knew what I had to do.

Back at class I took a sledgehammer and destroyed the broken mirror. I ripped out every inch of the inside of that box. I peeled off the red, the yellow, the black paint. I tore it out of my life. I wanted to start over. I could have just gotten a new box to start over, but that box had become me. I had to work with what I had, just like we all have to play the cards we're dealt. So I scrupulously tore out all I'd done. I cut the wire and ripped it out. I peeled off the glue. I left the slits that remained from the mirrors pushing through the lid because those wounds were still a part of me. But I wanted to begin again. I painted the inside of the box pure white, starting over. I began to refill the

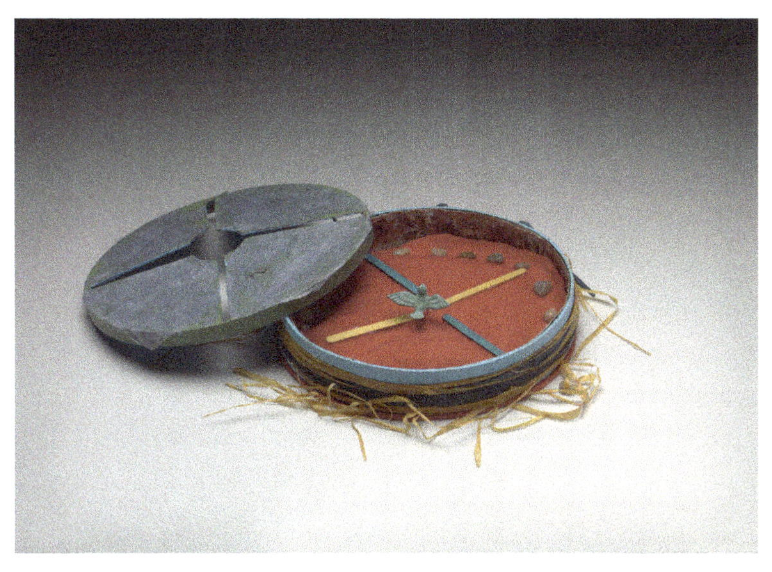

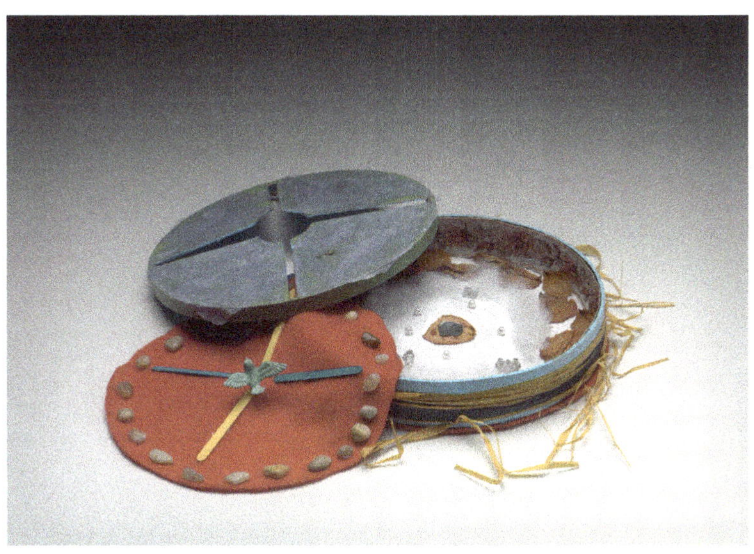

box, this time with expressions of love and compassion. I would take care of this fear once and for all.

I carefully placed a layer of red felt on top of the new white paint, a protective coating (page 77, top). On top of that, I lay colored sticks depicting the four directions. In the center, I glued a beautiful bird flying skyward. Stones surrounded the soft red fabric, symbolic of my own strength and my connection with nature. I cut slits in the lid to echo the four directions inside, thus opening the box up but still protecting it. I left remnants of the gold and blue taffeta originally tied around the box as reminders of the fear I still wanted to control.

Finally! I felt vindicated, pure. Reborn. I covered it all with a thin sheet of white gauze as a light protection. It was done. I could breathe again (page 77, bottom).

I wish I could say that was the end of the story, that fear no longer rules me. But, not long after I so carefully and intently routed fear from my life, words were said that brought my anxieties to the surface once again. And I realized that fear wasn't something I could simply be done with. It was something I'd have to continually cleanse myself of.

In this spirit of cleansing, we closed the fear project with a water ritual. Water is a powerful symbol of life, renewal, and purification in so many traditions. After sharing our work and what we'd learned, we considered our fears and wrote them on stones. Passing a rough sponge and a bowl of water from woman to woman, we scrubbed our stones clean, washing our fears away. We then wrote upon our stones once more, this time, our antidotes to fear. These we wrote in permanent ink, never to be expunged.

We shared our antidotes and our hopes. And whenever we see water, wash our hands, shower, or feel the rain, we can remember, and wash our fears away once again.

Sitting on the rock watching the river. The sky pure blue, the water flowing easy. Out a bit, I see a break in the silky stream, a riffling in the water. Curious. But now it's a foot-wide gash of rough water, lengthening and reaching toward me. Weird. I wrack my brain, a creature racing below the surface? I'm unnerved. It keeps getting closer, and suddenly it's upon me, and I'm thrown backwards by the force . . . of the wind.

RIVER LESSON: *It's hard to fathom what can't be seen*

WHEN THINGS ARE NOT WHAT WE THINK

Often when we create a new piece of work we believe we understand its meaning, only to step back and discover that it reflects a deeper truth. That was what Faith and Amy experienced as we explored the concept of "vessels."

We began the project by looking at definitions of "vessel": a container; a ship; an artery; a person infused with a quality of grace or godliness. The women sketched their initial visions as possibilities for their artwork. Then we looked at vessels created by other artists: the miniature sculptures of Ron Nagel; the torn-apart ceramic forms of Peter Volkous; Elizabeth Lundberg Morisette's creations from found objects. As we studied the other artists' pieces, I could see these images eclipsing the women's earlier vessel visions.

In a guided meditation, I invited the women to consider the vessel they would create: "Is your vessel soft? Hard? Are there sharp edges? Is it whimsical? Is there something inside? Is it bold, with dramatic colors? Light, with pastel shades? Is it made of clay? Fabric? Wire? Think of yourself as the vessel you are, with all the tastes, textures, thoughts, feelings, memories that your body holds within."

I ended with a quote from Jacquelyn Small: "We are not human beings trying to be spiritual. We are spiritual beings trying to be human."

As the women opened their eyes, I could see that dormant potential had been awakened.

Faith, a master yoga teacher, is intuitive by nature. When she makes art she likes to rely on her instincts. Her work is usually brightly colored, fun. She tells me her art makes her happy. She's often joyful as she works.

Faith started by picking up a small plastic bowl and bright pink paper. She began to decoupage the paper onto the bowl, working without pre-planning, allowing to come what might. When she was done, she felt she'd created a nest. She took it home. Her dog tore it up.

Faith arrived at the next class ready to begin anew. She had brought a balloon and a roll of string. Her plan was to shape a woman from them. She tied the string around the balloon to create a waist. She collaged paper onto the balloon, and, over that, fabric, layering her "woman" (right).

Later, when she was done, she opened her journal. As she started to write, she instantly grasped the real meaning of her piece: she had not made a woman as she had intended and believed she had. Her writing uncovered the truth: she had created a womb. She thought back to the initial piece, the one her dog had torn apart, and a deep knowing flowed through her: both pieces were nests. Or, as she now realized, each piece was a womb.

As Faith continued writing, the meaning of her sculpture

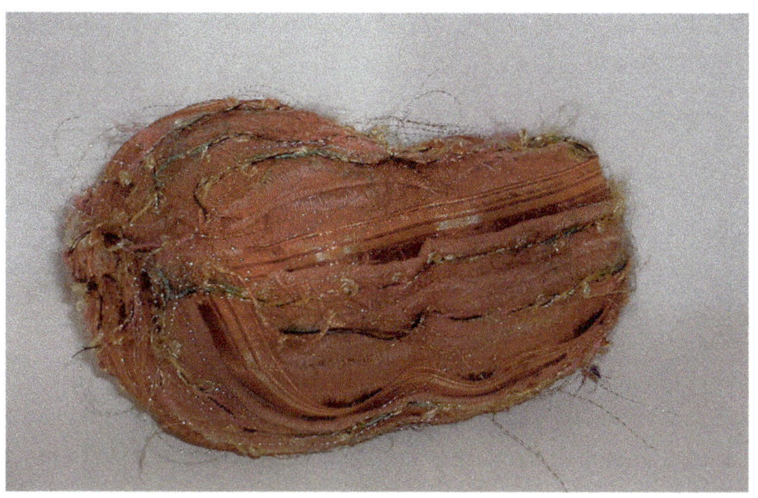

became clearer still. During sharing, she talked about what she'd discovered. "Over the summer I had a hysterectomy. It left me with this sense of profound loss. Everyone tried to make me feel better, telling me things like: 'It's fine – you don't need your uterus anymore,' and 'you weren't going to have any more children anyway.' But I was still filled with grief."

Faith told how disheartened she was to lose these female organs, and, moreover, that sense of possibility. Even if she wasn't planning to have more children, the promise was still extant. But with everyone around her telling her it was fine, she felt stifled from grieving. And so, it came out in her artwork. There, in the woman she'd planned to create, she had lovingly recreated her own womb.

As she kept writing, more was revealed. A second reminiscence also spoke through this piece. Some twenty-six years before, Faith had suffered a miscarriage. Then too, grieving had felt taboo, with others' gentle admonishments:

"Don't worry — you'll have another baby." Longing to mourn, she was blocked, and buried the pain. Here, a lifetime later, was her baby, her womb, and the love and grief she'd been carrying deep inside for twenty-six years. Finally, through her art and her writing, she could see it, share it, understand and embrace it. As she told us all of this, she instinctively, unconsciously, cradled her recreated womb like a baby, her story coming full circle.

Amy's exploration of vessels also unexpectedly led to secrets of the womb. A loving mother of three young children, Amy often talks about her kids and her hopes for them. Hers is a close family — the kids laugh and play together, and she and her husband do their best to make a happy home.

As she squeezed the clay between her palms, the vessel Amy was forming was a boat, maybe a canoe (right). In it she decided to place her three children. She formed a small child and affixed him in one side of the boat. She formed another and placed her on the opposite side. Something about that didn't feel right — her kids were so close-knit, she thought. The children should have been on the same side of the boat, together. So she adhered her three children together, and placed them on one side of the vessel. But somehow it felt wrong to remove the child she originally placed on the other side, so she left him there, alone. Three children on one side of the boat, and one on the other.

After a couple of classes, Amy completed the piece and began to write. That's when she arrived at a realization. She explained during sharing: "As the words flowed, the meaning of the fourth child was just immediately there. As a young woman, I had an

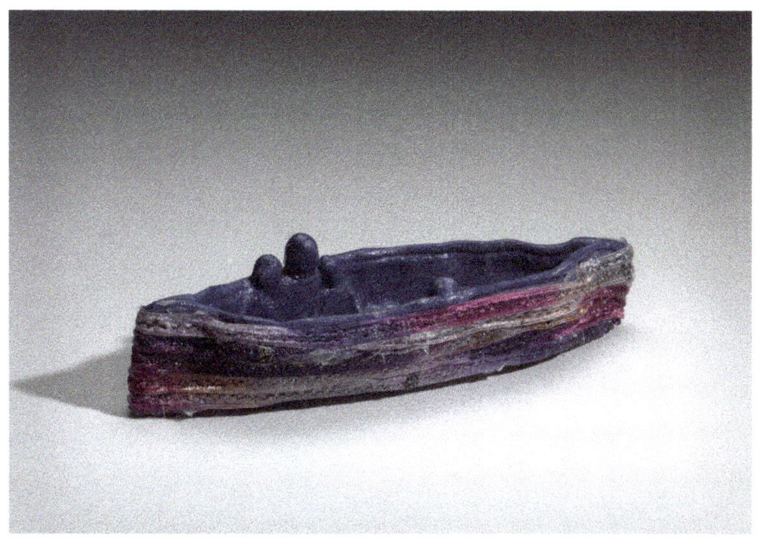

abortion. That's him — on the other side of the boat. That's why I couldn't just take him out. Somehow he's still a part of me and this family."

As with Faith's womb, Amy's canoe was not what she had thought. She discovered a much deeper and more complex truth.

The truths that Faith and Amy unearthed had lain submerged for years. While in that unseen place, however, these truths surely must have informed and propelled them at times, even without their knowing. By bringing these truths up from the darkness into the light of their present awareness, Faith and Amy were able to recognize and absorb them anew. And, though both of these instances were born of painful memories, both women were joyful. Their discoveries allowed them to recover parts of their lives they'd forsworn, and own them as theirs again.

Not too high above me I hear a bird jumping along a branch, attracting my attention. She's not a particularly striking bird and I lose interest. A moment later, she takes flight. I'm surprised, awed, by her brilliantly hued wings as they ride the air.

RIVER LESSON: *Our true colors are revealed when we open our wings and fly*

Finding one's voice

Rose came to one of my weekend retreats with a good friend. She'd come a long way, from Wilmette, Illinois, to spend the weekend making art and doing yoga in Madison, Virginia. During introductions, Rose shared with the group that she grew up in a house filled with beautiful artwork created by her mother, a successful painter, and her sister, now a professional sculptor. When people would visit, Rose's mom would gesture around and say, "This is my artwork, and this is Joni's sculpture, and this is Rose. She's good with people." It's true, Rose said, she was good with people — in fact, she is now a practicing therapist.

But what she had always longed to do was paint. She told us that she loved thinking about color and even dreamed about painting. She'd taken up the potter's wheel for a while, since that felt safely removed from her mom's and sister's domains, but it didn't satisfy. In the shadow of her mother's and sister's beautiful artwork, and her mother's critical eye, she always felt unworthy. She grew up with a deflated sense of not being good enough to make art of her own.

Our retreat was a weekend of art making. We had large wooden structures, canvases, and small, thirty-by-twelve inch shutters to work with. Rose chose one of the shutters, and asked me to help her get started with it.

"I want to make a blue painting," she said. "It's what I've been dreaming of." So I handed Rose a palette, and she squeezed out a bit of cobalt blue, a little cerulean, and some phthalo blue. I had her add some white and some raw umber to round things out a bit. She walked over to her area and painted her shutter in shades of blue. She removed a square insert near the top, and said she wanted to cover it in canvas so she could create a small "Marc Rothko-like painting" with floating colors of rectangles. But she was afraid to start. We talked a bit. To take the pressure off, I suggested she show me what she was thinking by painting it in her journal. A short time later, she came to me, journal in hand, beaming happiness. There it was, an exquisite painting, Rothko-esque and effortless. "Okay, you can go home now." I told her, "You're a painter. This is you, in your art, when you let go of judgment and fear."

Rose was ecstatic. She turned the shutter over and began again, creating three new paintings on the reverse side (right). She came back for a little more advice, nervous that choosing the wrong background color could ruin the piece. I suggested she see what the piece was asking for, what it needed, and she went back to work. Later she showed me. It had needed blue. She was thrilled as she absorbed the moment. Glowing, she told me, "I've created my blue painting!"

When MJ first came to the class she looked a little like a deer in headlights. From the very first project, she lamented an absence

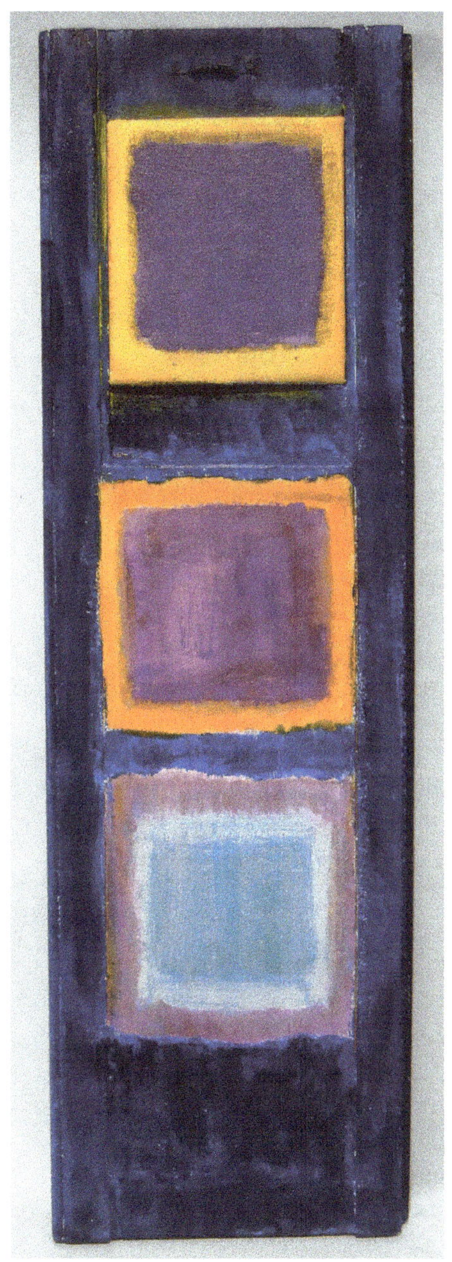

of ideas. During the weeks that followed, using the inventive collagist Joseph Cornell as our inspiration, we fabricated wooden frames and created mixed-media assemblages. The women were inspired and, with quiet deliberation, combined bits and pieces of fabric, words, and found objects into their personal Cornell-like containers.

MJ cogitated as she worked. She told me, more than a few times, "I have no ideas. I just don't know what to do." She persevered however, and her piece, with a clay shell as the focal point, was reminiscent of an ocean scene. Still, she didn't feel connected with it, and I could feel her frustration. She continued coming to class, though, slogging through her search for "ideas."

One week we embarked on a project using simple cardboard boxes. Something about this project got MJ's juices flowing. She cut away at the box, and soon her piece lost any inner or outer differentiation, becoming an overflowing sculpture. Colored lengths of fuzzy pipe-cleaners flowed to and fro, circulating from the inside out and back again, the tendrils of her box reminiscent of the arteries and veins flowing through a human body. Elatedly departing the studio that day, she exclaimed, "I have too many ideas – I think I'll have to do a bunch of these boxes!"

With that, MJ crossed the threshold into a new realm of her creativity. Her confidence began to grow. Everyone in the class could feel the transformation. She had found herself in her art. Even her family noticed the change. Her thirteen-year-old son, seeing her work on her art at home, "got into the act," she told us. He began crocheting, which he had learned, unbeknownst to her, from a friend's mother.

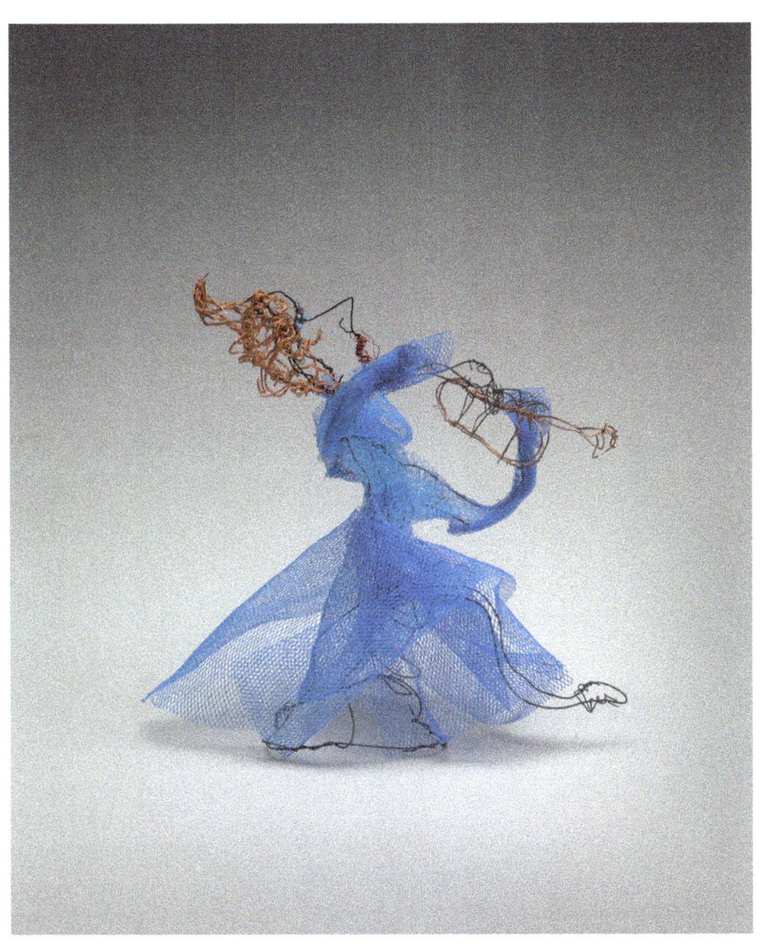

Then, one project in particular took MJ to a brand new place in her life and work. We were working with wire, this time inspired by the wiry stabiles of the amazing Alexander Calder.

MJ wound and knotted the thin wire, creating a standing figure of a woman. Using netting that had once held avocados from the grocery store, she clothed the woman, giving her personality and a whimsical warmth (page 95). She went home, made another wire figure, and then another. She crafted a life-sized woman to sit by her tub. MJ was so enthralled with her new medium that she decided to pursue her wire work on her own, creating a legion of wire people and, from there, wire masks.

Some time later I received an email from MJ, with the subject line "Art Exhibits":

Dear Lauren,

I just want to let you know that I got two masks accepted into the Strathmore Juried Art Show! I also had a piece in their Valentine's show.

Also, Lauren, I am going to have my own exhibit at the Potomac library for the month of April!

And a couple of months later:

Lauren:

Just thought I would let you know that I had a piece accepted in another juried exhibition. It is for the 4th of July celebration — at the Village of Friendship Heights — through Aug 2.

Also, the American Antiques Arts Association, which meets at the Ratner Museum, wants me to give a presentation about my work.

There's a medium for everyone. Sometimes it's just a matter of finding it, and through it, your voice.

Settled on my rock, watching the water rush by. The Mallards glide along, paired off, male and female. Way out in the river a Great Blue Heron stands, still as stone. She is peering into the water, watching, waiting. Wiley, still a puppy, is with me, and we are working on his "stay." I consider the heron. Motionless . . . patient . . . perfect. She sits that way for many minutes; really, for as long as we are there. As we sit, I remind Wiley to stay. And he does, for some seconds. He stands. I repeat the stay, and he does. He lies down, stays. A bit forlorn, but stationary. And as I watch the perfectly motionless heron and take in her stillness, I see, out of the corner of my eye, my little Wiley, slowly, quietly, surely, creeping away, nose sniffing eagerly as he stretches himself out, more and a little more, slinking away bit by bit . . . .

RIVER LESSON: *A dog is not a heron*

Liberating the Past

Women can be very hard on themselves. Hey, it's hard to be perfect. Constantly inundated by messages from our consumer-crazed culture, we conclude there is a lot that's not okay about us: the color of our hair, the length of our eyelashes, what we wear, and of course, the always ubiquitous . . . shape of our bodies. With big business as our judge and jury, many of us find it difficult to accept ourselves as we are. The verdict is in: we're not good enough.

But it's hard to be something you're not. And it's demoralizing to have it relentlessly thrown in your face. For many women, this implacable condemnation in magazines, TV, billboards, and movies has been internalized as an inner critic. We haul these feelings of insecurity around with us, whether to the supermarket or to an art class.

For many of us, though, mindsets of inadequacy hark back to childhood. Never feeling good enough. For some of us, a self-effacing internal dialog is an ingrained habit practiced over many years. It becomes a groove in our brain, like a groove in an old record, interminably reminding us of our shortcomings — or supposed shortcomings.

It's very difficult to proceed with this inner judge constantly questioning and harassing. So, oftentimes, this self-judgment is the first miasma we must move through on our way to making art that is Real. Quieting the incessant rant of an inner critic is essential to being able to listen within.

One very effective way to *out* our inner critic is by writing. When we expel our fears and insecurities on paper, the inhibiting words are no longer hidden away in a maze of confusing old beliefs. There is nowhere for the words to hide. Sometimes just exposing them on paper lessens their power over us. Other times the writing leads to more exploration and deeper understandings. By writing, we can look the critic in the eye and show him the door, if only for a little while.

And sometimes it's the work itself that frees us.

Stephanie came to me for a private session. She'd had some hard knocks in her life. As a girl in Germany she was taught to be hard on herself, and she learned it well. As an adult, she spent a lot of time and energy trying to right her life, and herself, reading, doing therapy, and learning about different spiritual paths and beliefs. She observed: "I spend too much time in my head."

She showed me a drawing she had done a long time before, a drawing of a dream. There were two dark figures: one who carried someone on her back; someone, Stephanie said, who she herself had killed. A dark binding went round and round them both, squeezing them together always. She told me, "This is the way I go through life, carrying this burden." Also in the dream drawing was a young girl offering flowers to the carrier figure.

Stephanie said she had spent much time considering this dream. "I know that I am all three of these figures."

She continued talking, sharing that sometimes she felt rootless, like she had "no feet." She thought that as a way to feel more grounded, maybe she should draw a tree. I contemplated the idea, and responded, "Let's first write a bit."

As I wrote, I realized that Stephanie's energy wasn't in the tree she thought she should draw. It was in the dream drawing she'd initially shown me. I asked if it would be okay for us to do our work around that. She was game. I brought out colored clay for her to recreate the scene from her dream, being sure to include colorful blocks in addition to the darker shades I knew she'd gravitate toward.

She began her work purposefully, shaping the clay into the figures from her dream. Her breathing intensified as she worked the figures. In short order the figures were complete: the little girl offering her flowers; the two figures, one grey, one olive green, both bound together with black bands. Stephanie's dream was there, in tangible form. "Wow, it's so powerful to see them really here." She was moved to see her dream come alive before her eyes.

I asked her to write about how it felt to create the scene, to write to each figure, and to learn what they each had to tell her. She set it all down on paper, writing furiously.

We talked. "The girl didn't have much to tell me. I already knew what she was about," she said. "But the burden — I'm so surprised at how much the burden had to say. And you know, I feel different about them now. I don't really feel like they're me any longer. No," she said quietly, thoughtfully, "they're from the past."

Stephanie's work had taken her to the precipice of a vital revelation. In times like these I sometimes suggest creating a follow-up piece, which can illuminate and fortify the fresh insight. In this situation, it seemed that altering her present piece would be an even better way to move forward.

I proposed a guided meditation. In the meditation, I asked Stephanie to consider how the figures might change if she let them — how she might alter them. When we were done with the meditation, she looked at the clock and said, "I don't think I can do any more today. This is already so much to take in." But there was to be more that day, more of immense value.

She was afraid to alter her piece. She'd lived this way for so long, it was her story. It was where she lived. "I think I'll just leave it as it is, as a kind of memorial," she said.

I asked her, "A memorial to what?"

"To what used to be," she answered. Hmmm . . . We talked some more, about how something had shifted for her, how I could feel the new compassion she felt for herself and for the weight she'd been carrying. Her tears flowed. "It's so amazing you would talk about compassion. It's something I really struggle with."

And then she said, "I think I would like to change it, but after talking and being in my head again, I don't know how to get back to that place of not thinking, that place of working from my intuition." I suggested she reread what she'd written earlier, and as she did she fell right back into following her inner guidance. She picked up her two bound figures. I had imagined that she would unbind them, free them, but instead she began to squash them together: the burden, the figure carrying the burden, and the binding. They began to blend, the gray of one figure, the olive green of the other, and the black of the bands that had held them together. As her palms worked them together they began to be one. And then, slowly but with sureness, they became a tree, with strong sprawling roots, and leaves reaching up to the sky. "New growth," she declared with a deep sigh.

Claire has taken the class many times. As a published author of three books and a professional editor, Claire is a successful career woman with a husband and two almost-grown children. A soft-spoken, kind, and thoughtful person, I have grown very fond of Claire, as many people have. Nevertheless, a demanding and disappointing relationship with her mother has often been revealed in her artwork. During the sharing period at the end of class one day, Claire explained that though she had struggled throughout her life, she had never been able to satisfy her exigent mother, leaving her frustrated, guilt ridden, and seemingly forever compensating. Then one particular piece helped her break the cycle.

The piece was really two pieces. The first one was a low, open, circular box. Towering in the center was a tall black pole. Surrounding the pole, on the floor of the piece, were heaps of beautiful curios — fragments of hope and devotion: a charm that said "love," a tiny baby, seashells, a basket — all gifts of the heart (page 106). Claire described what the work meant to her. "The pole represents my mother, a dark black hole. The gifts surrounding the pole are all the things I have tried to give her throughout my life: affection and kindnesses, even grandchildren," she said with a laugh. Claire told us that, as she worked the piece, she could see, "each gift just hit the pole and

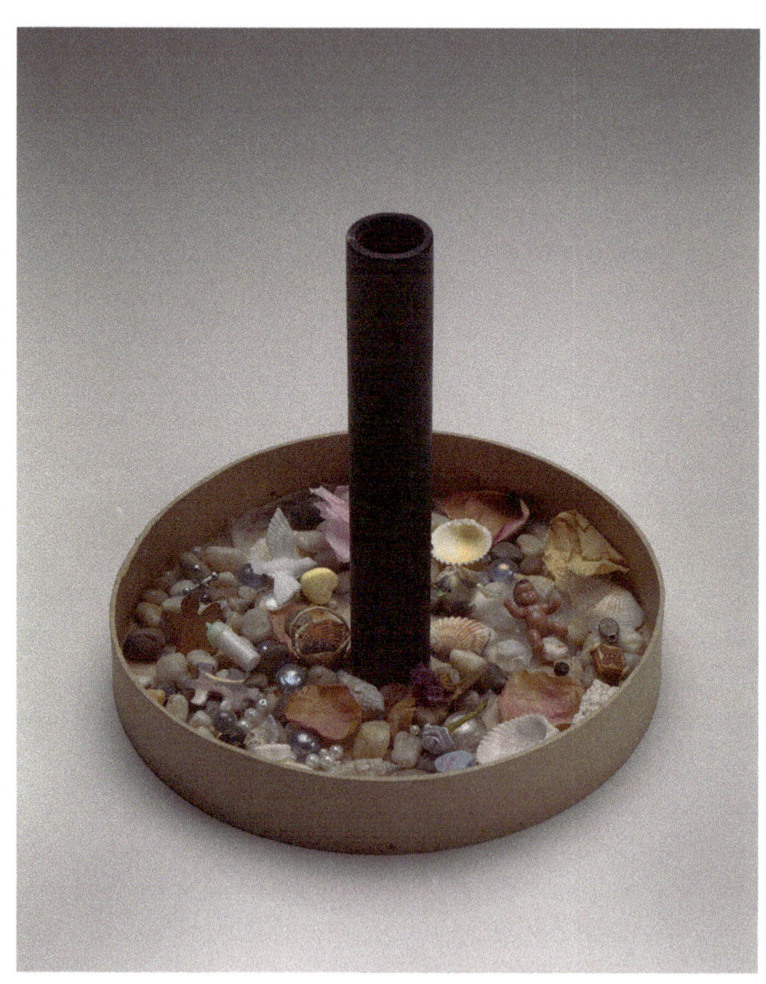

fell to the ground. And I realized my love bounces off the same way."

Claire explained how creating this tangible representation of her relationship with her mother was allowing her to finally let go of her urge to please her. Through her piece she came to a certain determination: it just wasn't possible. As she surveyed the gifts lying around the pole, she finally saw. She had done all there was to do. No more guilt, no more frustration.

Claire's project came to its culmination in the second part of her piece. It too was an open, round box. But inside resided a strikingly beautiful and mysterious bird, covered with exotic fabrics and colorful feathers. She was looking out from the box, standing on the edge, about to soar. Absolutely free (below).

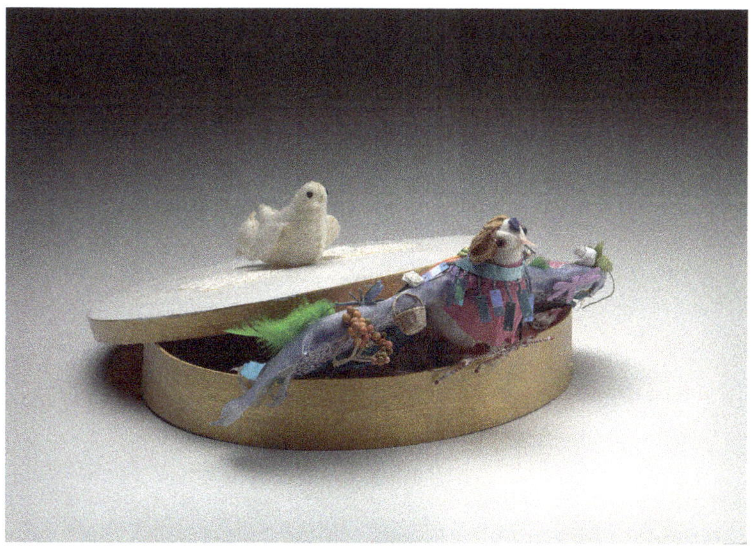

It's storming something fierce this morning. Rain and hail. The river careens. Debris, dragged under the churning brown water, rushes by. Huge logs jam up at the turns. I'm in awe of nature's power. But I too am nature — wherein lies my strength?

RIVER LESSON: *Seek, understand and step into your power*

Power

I'd been thinking a lot about the idea of power — not the kind that is displayed as political or corporate dominance on the world stage, but power in its most personal form. What does power mean to each of us, as women? Do we have power? Do we want power? How might we recognize power in our lives? And, to what end?

It began with a thought at the river: "What would it look like if I stepped into my power?" When I asked myself this question I felt instant anxiety. Even simply reflecting on power in conjunction with myself felt frightening and foreboding. And yet, it exhilarated me. I walked faster, completely absorbed in this scary and potent question: what would it look like if I stepped into my power? The question engaged me, and I decided to sit with it.

Over the days, during walks and meditations, I came to some conclusions. Power, in the way I'd been accustomed to thinking about it, had to do with might, with physical strength, with the capability to be "stronger-than." It had to do with war and fury, with anger and intensity and one-upmanship. This way of seeing power, I came to feel, reflected what I saw as a male perspective, revealed through the attitudes and behaviors of a predominantly patriarchal culture. I could see that I'd been looking at power from one angle, the one I was raised with, both in my home and within my culture.

As I thought about it further, I realized that in my experience many men owned their power, while many of us women continued to embody submission and endurance, or use our power quietly and even covertly. Times have changed and women do have more overt power than ever — here in the United States, anyhow — but there are still many ways we quietly veil our power, to make it acceptable. I decided that I was interested in coming out of the closet and living in my power. But what is that, exactly? What might happen if I unveil my power? What would that look like? What is the essence of my personal power?

This inquiry into women and power seemed a valuable one to bring to the classes. I asked the women to consider what power meant to them. I posed the question I'd asked myself: "What would it look like to walk in your power?" Very frank and even heated discussions ensued. More than one of the women found the idea of power too uncomfortable to contemplate and wished we weren't having the discussion. "I hate talking about this. It just feels scary." It still felt foreign to many of us. But did we not deserve to walk in our own power? And what, exactly, did that mean for each of us?

I chose the artist Marisol as an exemplar of an artist in her power. Marisol is a wonderful sculptor and a laudable role model. To make her art she carves huge blocks of wood, sometimes drawing or painting on them, leaving much of them in big block-like forms. It's large, physical work that uses humor and strength to create pieces of intimacy and power. We looked at much of Marisol's work at the beginning of class. I then handed everyone blocks of wood, carving tools, clay, and other materials to begin our work with power as our jumping-off point.

Lea is a fun woman with sparkling blue eyes and a quick laugh. I had no idea when I first met her that she held a high-level position in the mortgage industry, a job that's "all about numbers and finances, with very little straying outside the box." She treasures her time making art, living a little in the right side of her brain.

Knowing Lea, it was no surprise that her take on women and power would be lighthearted with a twist of irony. Her mixed media piece was of a woman with the face of a girl. She was sitting on some suitcases, looking a bit exhausted. There was a high-heeled shoe up in the air and a few too many legs for one person (page 114).

With a job like hers, and being a wife and mother with two daughters, Lea found the question of women and power compelling. She shared: "As a child, my parents made me feel that I could be anything. I loved to play 'career girl.' I had a suitcase I would load up with important things to take to important places and pretend I was going off to work. So, initially, I was thinking that power is being told you can be whatever you want to be. That's why I started the piece with the face of a girl."

But as she got going, there was more clarification. "The reality is that, as a woman, you end up filling so many roles. You're always running; that's what the legs are about." I was thinking: "How many legs can I possibly have and in how many directions

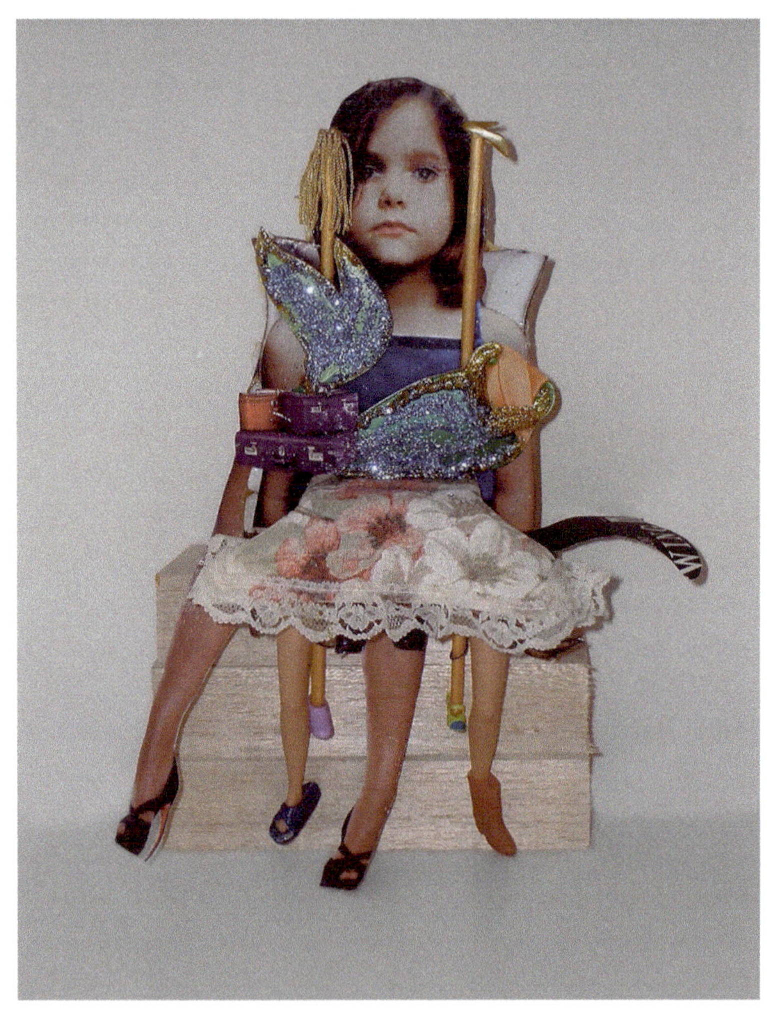

can I go? I mean, who could really walk if you had all these legs? You'd be stumbling all over yourself," she laughed.

Lea told me that this piece was a special one. "After class, I usually go home and don't talk. I'm in kind of a dreamy place. I usually won't show things to my family right away," she said. "But I shared this piece as soon as I got home, because it came from deep inside me and because it speaks to what it's like to be a woman. There's a fun aspect to it too. My husband was like, 'Okay . . . whatever . . . , ' but the girls . . . they loved it!"

As one who'd known abuse from an early age, Jess had a hard time feeling her own power. The idea of claiming it was challenging, but Jess' quiet patience and deliberate openness ultimately led to a valued insight.

Jess chose to work with a rectangular piece of balsa wood. She took a chisel and a knife, and before long the blank block had two large eyes carved into it. The eyes were shut tight. "The project took me back to not seeing with my own eyes," she said. "I used to spend all my time trying to imagine what other people were seeing. I was afraid to be myself and instead tried to appear a particular way to others. It was kind of a way of disappearing."

She added colorful wire and beads to her piece. But it wasn't right. She went back to carving. She looked at the eyes and started to round them out some more. As she worked, whittling away the slivers of wood, something unexpected started to happen. Jess saw that the eyes were beginning to open. Shaving by shaving the eyelids unpeeled, until finally, they were open wide (page 116).

Our art reflects our life. Jess' carving of the closed eyes and their slow but sure opening was like riding along a timeline of her life. From her loss of power at the age of twelve through the intervening years, Jess had carefully stayed invisible. She imagined that if she kept her eyes closed, no one would see her, and she would be safe. But now, here she was, an adult with the choice to open her eyes and retake her power. As Jess said, "I unlocked a piece of myself I didn't even know was there."

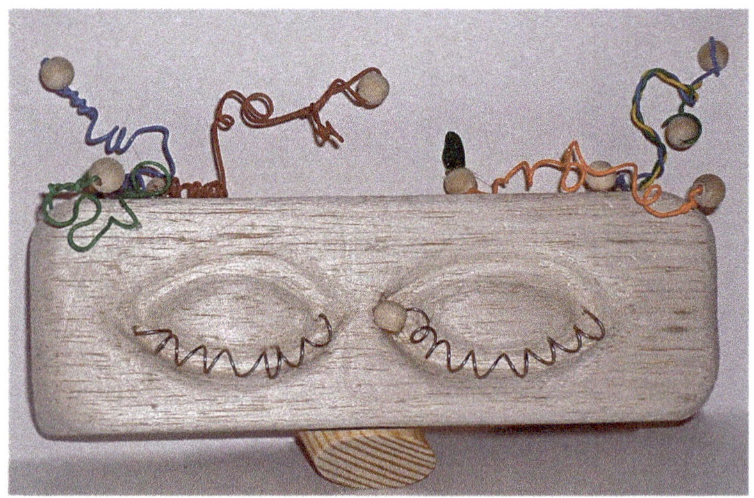

The light is soft this early morning. The trees warm and begin to bud again. On the Virginia side of the river they're bathed in a heavenly glow. Turning to the Maryland side, the scene is even more striking. The higher trees are lit, the lower still hidden from the sun, in a breathtaking blend of luminosity and shadow.

River lesson: *Without darkness there is no light*

GRIEVING AND HEALING

Where we are in any given moment of our lives is naturally confessed in our artwork. When we're joyful and open, the colors and movement in our art reveal our elation. And when we're going through challenges, our struggles reverberate in the work as well. Sometimes it has a healing power, as I've seen many times with women struggling with illness and death.

Karen signed up for an eight-week session while her beloved father was ill, but by the time our first class rolled around he was gone. It was a very tough period for her and she wondered if it was still a good idea to take the class, feeling so sad and vulnerable. But she decided to come, having already carved out the time in her busy life.

We started a project based on the concept of time. Jotting down our thoughts on strips of paper, we put the strips in a jar and reached in to read each other's musings aloud:

"Lately I feel like time is flying by at warp speed."

"Is the flow of time a figment of our imaginations?"

"Time has a natural rhythm, an unstoppable cycle, and the cycle doesn't care how you feel about it."

I had everyone close their eyes to mediate on time. During the quiet, I put forth some questions on being present in this moment and on time over millennia. I queried: "What images, shapes, words, thoughts, feelings come to you about time? Does time feel like a roller coaster? Does it seem to ebb and flow like ocean waves? Is time a line, a circle, an oval? Can you see time in the falling of the leaves, the changing trees, the aging of your kin?" I started up the music, playing songs about time, and we were off.

Karen reflected on her relationship with time, remembering her final days with her dad. "I had been very conscious of time when my father was dying. We'd spend the day in the hospital with him. He was unconscious but my brother Jay and I took turns reading *Treasure Island* to him, a book he'd always loved and read to us when we were little. We were hoping the sound of our voices might awaken him so we might reconnect once more."

Karen recalled the nightly drives from the hospital back to their old family home. Jay's and Karen's mom would sit in the front seat; Karen would sit in the back. "On the way home I would look out the car window, watching the moon. On our first night there it was huge, but as the nights went on, I saw it gradually shrinking. We were very conscious of it, Jay and I, and we talked about it. We were connecting my father's death to this natural cycle."

Karen gathered up some materials with that moon in her mind. By the third day of the project her piece was complete (right). She created a black-and-white tissue paper collage on wood, which replicated the phases of the moon. A small, square mirror was set in one of the crescents. Karen told me that the tiny mirror represented her beloved father looking down to her, and she looking back up to him.

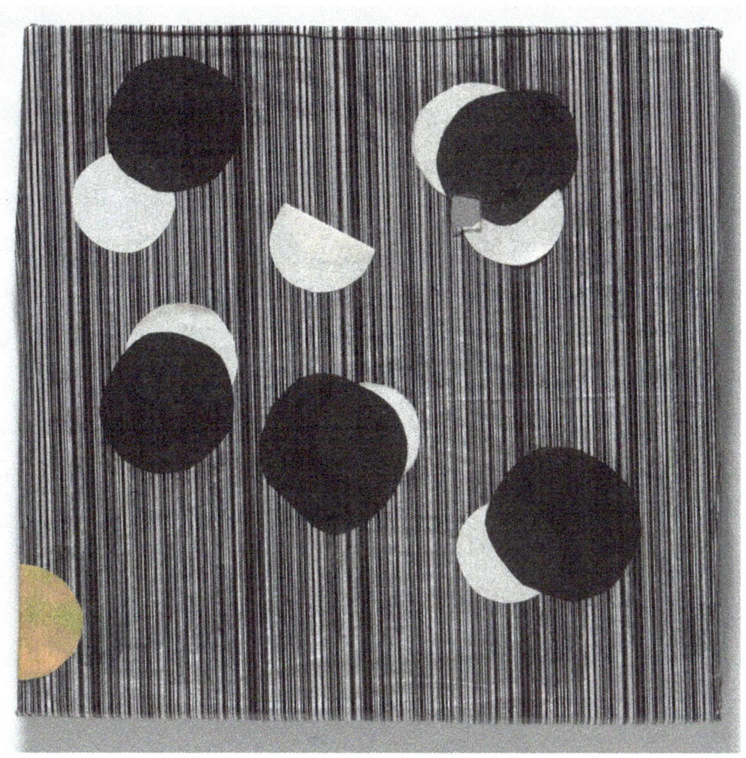

Karen was grateful to be able to process her father's death in this deep and meaningful way. She talked about it: "There's a natural rhythm to life and death, but it's hard to think of that rhythm stopping. And maybe it doesn't stop. Maybe it's like the phases of the moon: always coming back anew. But the truth is, I miss him. I think you never stop grieving. You just come to terms with it. You just have to say life goes on, remind yourself that this person is alive in me and in his grandchildren."

She went on, "I didn't understand how powerful the class would be in terms of processing my father's death. After the first day, I realized there probably couldn't have been a better time for me to take the class. I never would have had this tangible representation on that time in my life were it not for creating this artwork." Karen keeps her moon piece in a special place where she sees it every day, a photo of her Dad beside it.

In an all-day workshop on Valentine's Day, my plan was to let the group bask in gratitude and love, reflecting on those themes for the day. I'd picked up teacups and saucers at a local thrift shop to use as the foundation for the day's project. The jumping-off point stemmed from the phrase "My cup runneth over with love." Each woman chose a cup and saucer to work with. We wrote about them metaphorically: What do you have in the "cup" that is your life? What would you like to have in your cup? What would you like your cup to rest upon? What is your soft place to land? For fun and inspiration, we had a look at Meret Oppenheim's famous teacup: a cup, saucer, and spoon covered in fur.

As always, the idea was to get everyone's juices flowing and then to let go of thinking and allow the work to flow naturally.

Carla, a newcomer to the classes, was puzzled. She asked me what exactly I wanted them to do. I tried to clarify: "It isn't about what I want you to do. This is for you. I have no preconceived expectations." Other women who had attended the classes before nodded in understanding and reassured her. "I know just how you feel. I felt the same way at first." "Whatever you do will be right. Just let yourself explore." In a short while, I noticed Carla beginning to let down her guard and enjoy herself.

Some time later I looked up and saw that Carla had created a richly textured and beautiful world within her cup, filled with the warmth and love in her life. She had even altered her saucer into a soft place to land, covering it in rich red felt. But she had fastened a sheet of black opaque paper around both cup and saucer, making the piece dark, ominous. I knew that Carla was in the process of undergoing treatment for breast cancer. This dark paper enveloped her piece and brought it to a heavy and anxious conclusion. It felt like the dread of her cancer shrouded her piece and by extension, her life.

After a while, Carla looked up at me. "I don't like the dark paper around the cup anymore. It doesn't seem right, but we don't have a lot of time left and I've already glued it on . . . so I guess I'll just leave it."

My response was a gentle, "If it doesn't feel right to you, go ahead and change it." I tried not to sway her, just support what she was already feeling. She had to do what was right for her. I couldn't weigh in on her process, not at this point, anyway. But as she lifted off the black covering I could sense her relief from across the room. She went on to trim pastel-colored sheets of soft translucent paper into angular shapes. She glued them in its stead. She placed the freshly cut paper so that triangles of it actually peaked up above the rim, changing the shape of the cup itself, and lifting it into an ethereal space. Carla's piece was dramatically and conclusively altered. Hope was now in the place of fear. The soft light of the handmade paper cradled the cup and, by extension, Carla herself.

Carla's artwork directly reflected the ups and downs of her life. It allowed her, in the safety of a creative and compassionate space, to travel from darkness into light, symbolically and experientially.

The next day Carla sent me an email:

> *Thank you so much for yesterday. I had so much fun. What a day!*
>
> *What I want is for the cancer to revolve around my life and not the other way around. The experience I had with my piece shifted everything. It feels like I'm getting my balance back.*

I invited Kim for a private session as a gift. Her family had spent the past year struggling with her teenage son's diagnosis and treatment of a rare form of brain cancer, and I wanted to help her in some way. She was happy for a bit of a reprieve from doctors and hospitals, and eager to reflect on her experiences through art.

I wasn't sure what Kim would want to do with her time in the studio, but I wanted it to be just what she needed. As we talked, she related stories of her son Dave's bravery and strength throughout this terribly trying ordeal. She said, "I wish I'd written down all the extraordinarily mature and deep thoughts Dave has shared with me over the last few months." So we started with that. I left the room for a bit so Kim could have some privacy to write, thinking that she might be able to put down on paper some of Dave's words.

When I returned to the studio, we talked a bit more, and she spoke more about their difficult journey. In planning for the session, I had the idea that Kim might want to make a talisman, a sort of touchstone to help her through whatever challenges might lie ahead. But I wanted her to lead. I could hardly put myself in her place. Only she knew what she needed. I offered her a tray of multi-colored clay with some gentle guidelines for letting go, but no real suggestion as to what to do. She was consumed immediately. After a short while her piece was complete. With her eyes brimming with tears, she explained that she had created a replica of Dave as Superman, because, "He will have to be Superman to make it through this."

In the piece, her son had antennas reaching out from the top of his head. "The antennas represent Dave's uncanny ability to sense and soak in all the good that people send his way." Half a dozen arms surrounded him: "the many people who love and support him." And of course, a bright red Superman cape draped over his shoulders, evoking his super powers.

"It's funny," I said, "I thought it might be nice for you to make a talisman, and that's just what you did."

Later Kim wrote:

Lauren, I look at my talisman daily. Thank you so much for the time you spent with me; it really was healing. I'm off to Hopkins with Dave today. We're hoping for an easy week.

Some months and many difficult procedures later, Dave was on the mend. Kim's family and friends met up to participate in the Stride for Life 5K Walk / Run, raising money for the Childhood Brain Tumor Foundation. The name of their team? Naturally, Team Superman.

The seeds are carried by the birds, swept by the wind. The plants take root, stretch upward. Autumn. Leaves of vibrant colors waft gently from the trees above, landing where they will. When the cold winds blow, the water cools to ice. The snow falls. In time, the sun will warm, and the river will surge again.

RIVER LESSON: *The conditions are always right. Flourish*

Every day

We lead busy lives. Frenetic. Demanding. Rushing. We are assaulted, shamed, enticed, yelled at: Be more, Buy more, Need more. More MORE MORE!!! We're badgered into believing that we won't be happy until we have the biggest, the most, the best. But maybe, while we're hurrying to do more and be more, the real stuff of life is just sailing by, lost in the whirlwind.

What is it that makes a life? What is it that makes *your* life? Could it be the everyday moments that we sprint by on our way to the next destination? Could it be our normal, seemingly mundane days: being with family, seeing friends, a clear sky after the rain, a loving smile? I, for one, don't want my life to pass me by. I want to be present. I want to take in the beauty, the sadness, the joy, the wonder of my days. Hey . . . I don't know . . . maybe we do only live once, and I want to be awake and aware and take in all I can of the time I have on this earth.

In summer, when we take a break, I suggest to the women that, even though they won't be coming to my studio over the summer, they maintain their class time as sacrosanct, and continue taking this time for themselves to write, go to a museum, make some art, or just lie in the grass and watch the clouds blow by.

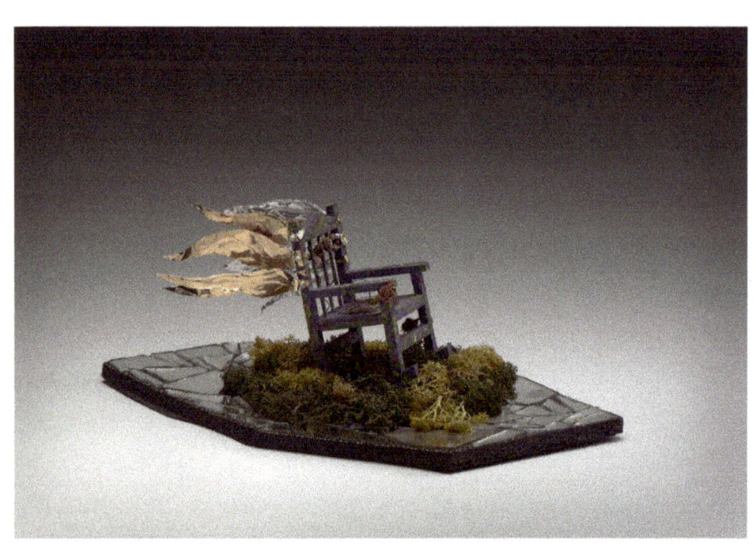

The moments that we take to do nothing at all can resound with the deepest meaning in our lives. If we're always running, when do we have awareness, when do we count our blessings, when do we take a measure of our lives?

This space we take for ourselves allows calm and contentment to flow into ourselves. And if we're lucky enough to create art, it can change how we see. As one woman wrote: "A whole new world of seeing beauty and loveliness has been opened up to me. Now I stop and gaze at something that I would have never noticed before. It's like finding a part of your mind that gets to go to a different place. It makes it easier to be in the world."

These moments allow us to see what's really important to us. When we take time to reflect, we remember what we love and treasure our days. We gain more appreciation for our lives and, in turn, have more to give to those we love and those we have yet to meet.

My wish for you, dear reader, is that you find your moments too, to listen to your inner voice, to see the golden glow on the trees at sunset. I hope you find time to observe how peeling paint on a building wall reveals color below, how beauty enters your heart and warms your very being. I hope that you write, that you paint, that you sculpt, that you create . . . that you explore all the riches that are you.

It is my dearest hope that through art we may each be empowered to realize our unique potential. And that we may each take that knowledge and the strength embedded in it to do what we can to help heal this difficult and beautiful world.

To all you are.

Endnotes

A little more about the particulars:

Planning projects

I think quite a bit about the projects we do and how to best introduce them. Inspiration for a project might come from a concept that seems valuable to delve into or a medium I'd like us to have an opportunity to work with. But whatever the medium or theme, I think it through with the aim of helping the women find their own way in to the project, an approach that will allay their fears and allow their inner spirit to emerge as effortlessly as possible. I have spent many a river walk pondering how to best present a project from launch to conclusion.

Jumping-off points

Jumping-off points are thoughts, concepts, or questions that I hope will have meaning for the women. One time the jumping-off point I offered was "turning points": moments that have altered our life's paths in some way. Sometimes these prompts come to me on river walks, ideas like "cocoons" or "balance," for instance. At the start of a project, we write about whatever the jumping-off point brings up, and then just let go of this initial idea completely. The writing is a kind of preparatory work. It's a way of getting the ball rolling, but we don't necessarily stick with the thoughts that emerge on the page. In fact, it's better when we just let them go and allow the materials and our instincts to guide us. Often the art will come full circle, back to the starting point, but there's no need for it to. There is a knowing deep down within each of us, and that's where the real seeds are sown.

Writing

I ask the women to write at least once a day, even when they're not in class. It doesn't have to be a lot of writing, just a touch of pen to paper. If there is more to say, it will come. Unlined journals encourage an expressiveness difficult to attain on a lined page; the size of the words and the feel of the letters correspond to the emotion at hand, and there's space for drawing or collage when words won't do. I encourage inexpensive sketchbooks, rather than fancy journals, so the book won't feel too precious for even the most vile thoughts and feelings.

The privacy of the journal is tantamount. It is one place where we can think and say unadulterated truths, with no repercussions. It is a sacrosanct space of complete and undiluted freedom. Just having this private sanctum to reflect on one's life has tremendous impact on our sense of freedom and possibility.

Incorporating nature

Oftentimes, our projects reflect the seasons, summoning the natural rhythms of life. We work around themes of rebirth and renewal in spring, cocooning and hibernation in winter, letting go in fall. It makes sense, and it feels right. We reconnect to the ebb and flow of nature, and in the process, to our own natural creative impulses.

Sometimes, in the spring, we draw outdoors. It helps to slow us down and reveals the natural world around us more deeply, sometimes as never before. The complexities even in one leaf are a miracle to behold. Our drawing stints bring musings like this one: "When I went walking this morning I noticed the seed pods on a red maple. After last week's drawing session I looked at these gifts of nature in a different way."

One thing naturally leads to another. Being in deeper touch with nature and her awe-inspiring intricacy and abundance leads us to gratitude. Being in touch with our own natural vision brings new awareness. The greater our awareness, the deeper the gratitude. The deeper the gratitude, the more soundly filled we are. And this fullness, this appreciation will emanate from us to touch each person we meet.

Materials

The choice of materials we work with is fundamental to the quality of the work that will be created. I choose our materials with great care. If we are using fabric, I consider the color options and quality of the fabrics for the specific project at hand. If you give people luscious materials and beautiful colors, they can't help but create wonderful pieces. A plethora of natural materials is always on hand — feathers, stones, branches, including whatever I find on my river outings.

Sharing

Sharing brings the process full circle. When we are hard at work, there is a busy hum in the studio, everyone deep in her own world. Hours fly by without a word.

We often work on projects over a number of weeks. Sometimes, we're so involved that we hardly look up. At the project's completion, we write, and then, we take time to share. Talking together about the work, the advent of its creation, and the experience of creating it is completely and necessarily optional. In order to work with total freedom, without worry about what other people might think, it's vital to know that our work will never have to be explained — to anyone. So whether to share at all, or to what extent, is completely discretionary. It's important to know from the start that this is in our own control. We may rely only upon what feels right at the moment.

Alexander Calder once said, "When an artist explains what he is doing, he usually has to do one of two things: either scrap what he has explained, or make his work fit in with the explanation." And in the usual making of art, I think that's true. But here, it's not really about explaining; it's more about exploring, pursuing a deeper understanding of the work, it's impetus, and our selves.

As strange as this might seem, even without any obligation, sharing by the women in the classes has been consistently unanimous and unequivocal. It is clearly too valuable a part of the experience to forgo. No one wants to miss out on voicing what they have garnered from their process, or on hearing her colleague's reflections about her work. Sharing has become a vital facet of the experience. Through talking together, we learn more about ourselves and how others see us and our work. The other women reflect ourselves back to us. This increased clarity about who we are is a great gift. As one woman once remarked to me, "We may know nothing about each other in the usual superficial ways, but we know each other's deepest truths, hopes and fears — the real person beneath the façade."

Sharing is a potent and rewarding conclusion to the threefold process of writing, creating, and sharing. It enriches our comprehension of the work and ourselves, and has led to ever deepening relationships within the groups, cherished friendships.

The therapeutic nature of making art

People occasionally comment that the classes sound like therapy. While I am not a therapist and I make that clear before the classes even begin, we do touch on intimate issues. But it is always each woman's choice how personal to make her work and how much to share. She can discard the jumping-off point if she likes and do whatever she pleases. It's all about her. The classes are not and have never been meant as a replacement for therapy. Nevertheless, many of the women find the classes to be therapeutic, as art so often is.

Acknowledgments

With Gratitude:

I have cherished working with the many women who've come to my studio through the years. Their willingness to risk and their steadfast support for one another have taught me so much. I especially would like to thank the women who were so generous in sharing their artwork and stories in this book so that others might know the many rewards of creativity. I will be forever grateful for their openness.

There are many more tales I could have told, many journeys we have taken together. I hope every woman who has shared something of herself in our classes knows that she too is reflected in these pages. I couldn't have told these stories without you.

I owe a great deal, too, to my parents, who continue to inspire me with their generosity and zest for life; to Robert and Andrew, my sweet and funny brothers, who cheer me on in all my endeavors; and to my treasured friends, who love and support me no matter what. My thanks especially to Karen Wise, my loving blood-sister for always, and to my Women Empowered circle, who have encouraged me throughout this project: Gail Chinoy, who nourishes me with her quiet wisdom and our many laughs; Marian Sherman, who is always, always there for me; Susan Orchin, my steadfast champion even from afar; Renee Butler, my buddy par excellance; Rebecca Petillo, who inspires through her work and words; and Maureen McRaith, whose beautiful energy will light up any room.

So many people have supported me through my years of teaching and making art; I could write a book thanking them. I hope they know my gratitude. I am indebted also to the many people who were kind enough to provide valued feedback on early drafts or otherwise help me navigate the path to publication, including: Abbey Alpern, Jennifer Attebery, Jaime Banks, Claire Bove, Flora Bowley, Vicki Breman, Nancy Brucks, Susan Buffone, Jill Cahn, Naomi Cahn, Ira Chinoy, Nancy Collamer, Lisa Courturier, Rachel Dack, Ursula Daniels, Rocky Delaplaine, Lissie Diringer, Whitney Freya, Paula Gorlitz, Mary Jo Harmon, Veronika Herman, Andrea Joseph, Jonathan Karp, Jean Lanham, Lisa Lauroesch, Tiffany Montavon, Randon Billings Noble, Arla Patch, Laura Perciasepe, Carol Prince, Megan Rader, Wendy Richmond, Meryl Rome, Michael Roth, Marc Sandalow, Judy Segal, Cecilia Simon, Alyson Stanfield, Sara Taber, Liz Thoburn, Maye Torres, Peter Vaslow, Mark Wise, Martha Young, and Judy Zimmer.

Christine Cote of Shanti Arts Publishing saw something special in my words, and touched me with her vision of this book as a gift of art. I'm truly grateful for her guidance, knowledge, and thoughtful editing. Working with Christine has been a process of true creative collaboration.

Most of all, I'd like to thank Elliot, Ty and Kaia, who heard all the ups and downs of this book for a good, long time, but rose up always to discuss, ponder, support, and guide. Their love is more than I could ever have imagined.

And finally, to our sweet pup Wiley, who was the truest of friends each and every day, and who lovingly taught me the difference between a dog and a heron.

Credits

Photos, pages 51, 61, 77, 87, 95, 106, 107, 123, 132: Mark Gulezian

Artwork, page 132: Rebecca Petillo

Photo, page 146: Kaia Diringer

Cover art by the author

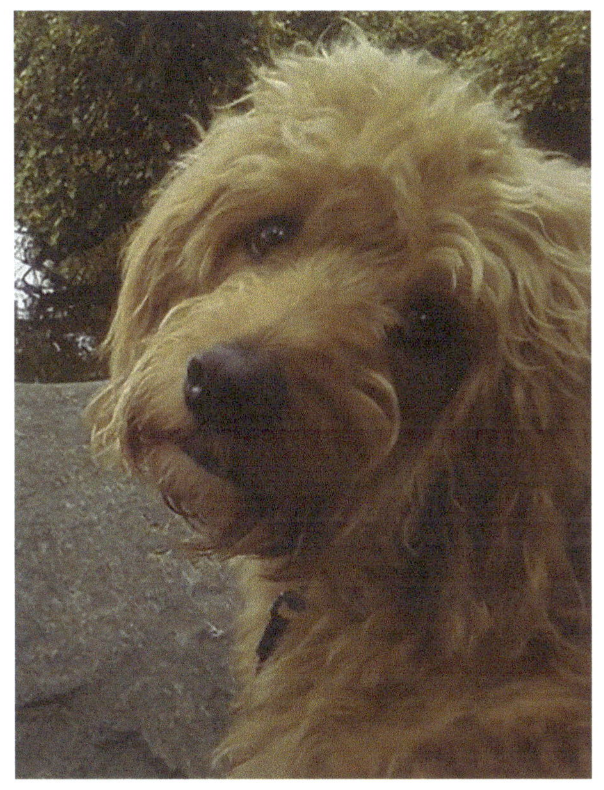

Wiley
2004 - 2015

About the Author

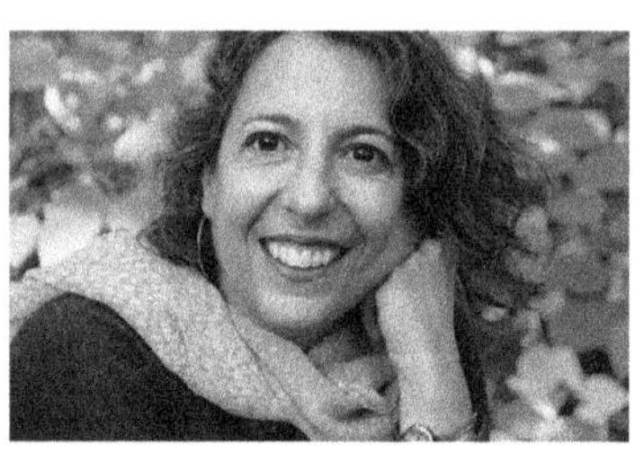

Lauren Rader is a lifelong artist and art educator. Her works in stone, clay, oils, and pastels have been exhibited in California, Colorado, Maryland, Massachusetts, Texas, Washington, D.C., and the U.S. Embassy in Fiji, and are in numerous private and corporate collections. Beginning as a teen arts-and-crafts counselor at her beloved Camp Cayuga, Lauren has introduced generations of children to the wonders of art. In 2005 she opened her art studio to adult students, offering classes for women called Releasing the Creative Powers Within. The women's personal and collective journeys into creativity became the inspiration for this book. Lauren currently resides in Bethesda, Maryland. To learn more about Lauren and her work visit www.LaurenRaderArt.com.

www.ingramcontent.com/pod-product-compliance
Lightning Source LLC
LaVergne TN
LVHW052354100826
845147LV00013B/834

* 9 7 8 1 9 4 1 8 3 0 8 9 5 *